taste.
SLOW COOKING

Over 100 mouth-watering recipes

igloo

igloo

Published in 2010
by Igloo Books Ltd
Cottage Farm
Sywell
NN6 0BJ

www.igloo-books.com
Copyright © 2010 Igloo Books Ltd

10 9 8 7 6 5 4 3 2
ISBN: 978 1 84852 839 0

Food photography and recipe development: Stockfood, The Food Image Agency
Front and back cover images © Stockfood, The Food Image Agency

Printed and manufactured in China.

contents.

introduction.

Slow cooking is the perfect way to cook up delicious, hearty meals for family and friends. Most of the work is done ahead, so you have time to enjoy your guests' company, put your feet up or even go out while dinner cooks away happily on its own. Many slow-cooked dishes also benefit from an even fuller flavor if cooked a day or so ahead, and then reheated.

These recipes offer the perfect antidote to fast and convenience food, setting out easy, step-by-step instructions so that you can create your own culinary masterpieces.

For many foods, though, there is an even stronger reason for slow-cooking and that is to achieve the deeper, richer, more complex flavors that long, slow cooking develops. The best examples of this are when cooking with meat. Prime cuts of meat, like fillet, are best cooked quickly to preserve their own innate tenderness, while the tougher, fattier (normally cheaper) cuts, like lamb breast and shank or beef brisket, really benefit from slow cooking, becoming tender and developing rich satisfying flavors. You can sit back as the wonderful aromas waft round the house when meat is simmering.

There are, of course, many classic slow-cooked dishes that don't include meat, such as Provencal ratatouille of peppers, aubergines, courgettes, tomatoes, garlic and herbs stewed in olive oil, in which the individual flavors all meld wonderfully into a rich sunny amalgam. Some vegetables, like red cabbage, fennel and celery, also have their own individual flavor brought out by braising in a little liquid. They are also richly aromatic.

There are also slow-cooked fish dishes, based on a long-cooked mix of vegetables, herbs, fish heads and trimmings and/or shells, which is strained and the delicate fish added to it at the end.

The long slow-cooking methods that give the best results are stewing, braising and pot-roasting. Stewing of meat - normally with added vegetables and herbs, and some liquid such as stock or wine - can be done in a casserole or tightly covered pan at a gentle simmer for an hour or two, in a low oven for roughly twice as long, or, of course, in a slow cooker. Braising and pot roasting are quite similar, but much less added liquid is used and the meat is usually first browned.

Slow-cooking has recently become fashionable among top chefs, who are advocating cooking meat at relatively low heat (about 65°C) for four to five hours to bring out the maximum flavor. Indeed, many chefs are now trying an entirely new method of cooking known as sous-vide (meaning 'under vacuum'), in sous-vide the food to be cooked is vacuum-sealed in a plastic pouch which is immersed in a water bath heated to a steady 60°C. For chicken, this is the exact temperature at which its proteins set but before they start squeezing moisture out of the meat fibers. This method brings out the full flavor and tenderness of the meat, but there is absolutely no possibility of the meat being overcooked.

Tips for slow cooking:

Brown the meat first, in batches if necessary. This will caramelize the outsides and some juices, which will help improve the final colour and flavour of the meat. Do this in the pot you plan to cook in, ideally a flameproof casserole with a tight-fitting lid.

Don't trim away all of the fat on the meat before cooking. The fat will contribute a lot of flavour and help make the meat tender. Any excess will rise to the surface of the cooking liquid, and can be skimmed away.

Toss the meat in a little flour before browning, pat it dry first with some kitchen towel to help ensure that only a very light dusting of flour clings to the outside. This will give your meat a good colour.

Only lightly season slow-cooked dishes at the outset. The long cooking reduces the cooking liquid and concentrates the sauce, so it can easily become too salty. Instead, adjust the seasoning at the end of cooking.

When simmering a stew, do it over a low heat so that the liquid bubbles only very gently around the ingredients. This will prevent the excess fat from emulsifying with the sauce, which might give a greasy finished dish.

Covering the dish with a tight-fitting lid or foil is very important, especially with braised dishes in which the meat is cooked in relatively little liquid.

Making a slow-cooked dish the day before will improve the flavour even more. Chill it overnight, then reheat and simmer gently for the briefest time possible before serving. If the dish is very fatty, this also gives you the opportunity to spoon off the solid fat on top.

The tempting slow-cooked recipes that follow will provide you with exciting dishes full of flavor using all sorts of foods suitable for a range of occasions from simple family meals and snacks to special occasions and entertaining guests.

soups
& stews.

Beef and potato stew

Prep and cook time: 1 hour 50 minutes
Can be frozen
Serves: 4

Ingredients:
800 g | 2 lbs onions, chopped
1 carrot, diced
12 small new potatoes, scrubbed clean
800 g | 2 lbs braising steak,
cut into bite size pieces
3 tbsp vegetable oil
2 tbsp tomato paste
4 tbsp paprika powder
1 tsp ground caraway
1 tbsp flour
salt
freshly ground pepper
500 ml | 2 cups beef stock

Method:

Heat the oil in a large pan and brown the beef on all sides. Set aside.

Add the onions and carrots to the pan and cook until tender.

Add the paprika, caraway and flour, pour in the beef stock and bring to a boil, stirring constantly.

Return the beef to the pan, stir in the tomato paste, cover and simmer gently for approximately 1 $\frac{1}{2}$ hours.

Season to taste with salt and pepper and serve.

Curried parsnip soup

Prep and cook time: 50 minutes
Can be frozen
Serves: 4

Ingredients:
600 g | 1 ½ lbs parsnips
1 large potato
1 shallot, chopped
1 tbsp butter
2 - 3 tsp mild curry powder
1000 ml | 4 cups vegetable stock
100 ml | 7 tbsp cream
Cayenne pepper
1 tbsp toasted sesame seeds

To garnish:
coriander|cilantro leaves

Method:

Peel and dice the parsnips and potato.

Heat the butter in a large pan and cook the shallot until soft.

Add the diced parsnips and potato and stir in the curry powder. Cook for 2 minutes.

Stir in the vegetable stock and simmer gently, stirring occasionally, for about 30 minutes.

Add the cream and puree the soup. Return to the pan and simmer to reduce slightly, or add a little more stock as necessary. Season to taste with salt and Cayenne pepper and ladle into bowls.

Garnish with Cayenne pepper and sesame seeds and serve sprinkled with freshly chopped coriander/cilantro leaves.

Lentils with tomatoes and pancetta

Prep and cook time: 1 hour 10 minutes
Cannot be frozen
Serves: 4

Ingredients:
150 g | ½ cup pancetta, diced
2 cloves garlic, chopped
2 tbsp fresh thyme
½ tbsp sage leaves, shredded
2 tbsp olive oil
400 g | 2 cups lentils
500 ml | 2 cups dry red wine
500 ml | 2 cups vegetable stock
6 peeled, tomatoes, seeded and diced
20 g | 1 cup fresh basil, chopped
white wine vinegar

Method:
Heat the oil in a deep skillet and fry the pancetta until crisp.

Take out about ⅓ of the pancetta and set aside. Add the garlic, herbs and lentils to the skillet and sauté briefly.

Add the red wine and stock, cover and cook for 30-40 minutes until the lentils are almost soft.

Add the diced tomatoes to the lentils, mix and cook for a further 10 minutes.

Season with salt and pepper and add a little vinegar to taste. Serve sprinkled with the basil and the reserved pancetta.

Oxtail soup with grilled cheese and chive bread

Prep and cook time: 2 hours
Can be frozen
Serves: 4

Ingredients:
3 onions, peeled
2 carrots, peeled
200 g | ½ lbs celeriac|celery root
2 tbsp vegetable oil
1 g | 2.2 lbs oxtail, cut into pieces
1 tbsp salt
4 cloves
2 bay leaves
1 tsp pepper corns
½ tsp juniper berries
soy sauce
2 tbsp chopped chives

For the toast:
4 slices of bread
40 g | ½ cup grated cheese
1 tbsp chopped chives

Method:
Chop the onions in half.

Chop the carrots and celeriac/celery root.

Braise the onions, cut side down, in a large saucepan over a high heat until dark brown. Remove from the pan and set aside.

Pour oil into the pan and fry the ox tail over high heat. Add the vegetables and continue to fry. Carefully pour in 1500 ml / 1 ½ quarts of cold water.

Slowly bring to a boil. Add the salt, cloves, bay leaf, pepper and juniper berries. Partially cover the pot with a lid and simmer over low heat for approximately 2 ½ hours.

In the meantime:

Preheat the grill.

Sprinkle the bread with the cheese and chives and grill for approximately 5 minutes taking care not to burn.

Strain the soup, skim the surface with a slotted spoon to remove any fat and season with soy sauce to taste.

Remove the meat from the bones and dice.

Divide the meat between the serving bowls. Sprinkle with the chives. Serve along with the toast.

Clam chowder

Prep and cook time: 50 minutes
Cannot be frozen
Serves: 4

Ingredients:
500 g | 1 lb clams
500 g | 1 lb floury potatoes
1 onion, chopped
2 celery stalks, sliced
3 slices bacon
2 tbsp butter
2 tbsp flour
350 ml | 1 ½ cups milk
150 ml | ⅔ cup cream
1 tsp thyme leaves
1 tbsp fresh, chopped parsley

Method:

Thoroughly wash the clams. Place them in a pot with 1 cup of water. Cover the pot, bring to a boil and shake the pot several times. Continue boiling for 3-5 minutes until the clams open. Discard any unopened clams.

Strain the clam water through a fine sieve, reserving the liquid.

Peel the potatoes and cut them into small cubes. Boil them in salted water for approximately 15 minutes and then mash.

Slice the bacon into strips.

Sauté the bacon, onion and celery in the butter. Sprinkle the flour on top. Continue to sauté and stir until the onion is translucent and the celery has wilted.

Stir in the milk, clam water and ½ cup water. Bring to a boil, reduce the heat and simmer for approximately 15 minutes.

Add the potatoes and clams to the soup, stir in the cream, thyme and parsley and season with salt and pepper.

Pour the clam chowder into the bowls and serve.

Chicken stew with peanuts and coconut

Prep and cook time: 1 hour 10 minutes
Can be frozen
Serves: 4

Ingredients:
4 chicken breasts, cut into bite size pieces
2 onions, finely chopped
3 cloves garlic, crushed
2 green chilli peppers, deseeded and cut into rings
1 tbsp curry powder
1 tsp freshly grated ginger
50 g | 1/3 cup ground almonds
4 okra pods, sliced
2 tbsp ghee
1/4 tsp ground cardamom
1/2 tsp ground cinnamon
1 1/2 tsp ground cumin
1 tsp ground coriander
400 ml | 1 2/3 cups coconut milk
300 ml | 1 1/3 cups vegetable stock
2 tbsp shelled peanuts

for garnish:
coriander|cilantro leaves
coconut shavings

Method:

Mix together the onions, garlic, chilli peppers, curry powder, grated ginger and almonds.

Melt the ghee in a pan, add the cardamom, cinnamon, cumin and ground coriander and cook for 1 minute.

Add the prepared onion and spice mixture and fry for 2 – 3 minutes, stirring.

Add the coconut milk, stock and chicken pieces and cook gently, without a lid, for about 45 minutes.

10 minutes before the end of cooking time add the okra.

Season with salt and sugar and stir in the peanuts.
Serve in bowls, garnished with coriander/cilantro and coconut shavings.

Irish stew

Prep and cook time: 2 hours
Can be frozen
Serves: 4

Ingredients:
800 g | 2 lbs mutton or lamb,
boned neck
2 large white onions
3 tbsp vegetable oil
600 ml | 2 ½ cups beef stock
2 bay leaves
800 g | 2 lbs floury potatoes
2 tbsp fresh, chopped parsley

Method:
Cut the meat into bite-sized pieces.

Peel the onions. Slice into thick rings.

Heat the oil in a large pot. Brown the meat in batches. Remove from the pot and set aside.

Add the onion slices to the pot and cook until translucent.

Put the meat back in the pot.

Pour in the beef stock and add the bay leaf. Cover and simmer over a low heat for about 1 hour.

Peel the potatoes and cut into eighths. Add them to the stew and bring to a boil over high heat. Turn down the heat and continue cooking over a low heat for another 30 minutes until the potatoes are tender.

Season to taste with salt and pepper. Garnish with the parsley and serve.

Ratatouille with rosemary

Prep and cook time: 40 minutes
Cannot be frozen
Serves: 4

Ingredients:
1 medium aubergine|eggplant
2 onions
1 green bell pepper
1 yellow bell pepper
1 red bell pepper
2 courgettes|zucchinis
2 cloves garlic
6 tbsp olive oil
1 tsp fresh, chopped rosemary
1 tsp fresh, chopped oregano
400 g | 1 lb tomatoes, diced
2 tbsp tomato paste

Method:
Remove the stem from the aubergine/eggplant and cube.
Salt the cubes and allow them to sit for 10 minutes.
Wash the cubes and pat dry.

Peel and slice the onion into rings.

Halve the peppers, remove the ribs and seeds and
coarsely chop.

Slice the courgettes/zucchinis.

Peel and slice the garlic.

Heat the oil in a saucepan or a pot. Sauté the aubergine/
eggplant, onions, peppers and courgette/zucchini.
After 5 minutes, stir in the garlic, rosemary, oregano, tomatoes
and tomato paste. Season with salt and pepper.

Cover and simmer for 10 minutes or until the vegetables are
cooked. Season to taste.

Blanquette de veau

Prep and cook time: 2 hours 30 minutes
Cannot be frozen
Serves: 4

Ingredients:
1 kg | 2 ¼ lbs veal shoulder, boned
2 veal bones
250 ml | 1 cup dry white wine
1 onion
4 cloves
2 carrots, peeled and halved
1 clove garlic, peeled
bouquet garni
(parsley, bay leaf, thyme)
1 tsp peppercorns
5 tbsp butter
400 g | 1 lb pearl onions, peeled
2 tbsp flour
lemon juice
1 egg yolk
100 g | ½ cup crème fraiche
2 tbsp fresh parsley, chopped

Method:
Wash the veal shoulder and pat dry. Place in a large pan together with the veal bones.

Peel the onion and stud it with the cloves. Add the onion, carrots, garlic, bouquet garni and peppercorns to the pan and pour in the white wine and enough water so that the meat and vegetables are covered.

Bring to a boil, skimming off any froth that rises to the surface, cover and simmer gently for 1 ½ hours or until the meat is tender.

Remove the veal shoulder from the pan, let cool a little and cut into bite-sized pieces.

Strain the cooking stock and set aside.

Melt 1 tbsp butter in a clean pan. Sauté the onions for 5 minutes, pour in a little of the veal broth, simmer for 5 minutes or until tender then set aside.

Heat 2 tbsp butter in a large skillet, fry the veal pieces on all sides until lightly brown and set aside.

Melt the remaining butter in a clean pan, add the flour and stir for 2 minutes. Add 4 cups of the stock and stir until thickened.

Mix together the egg yolk and crème fraiche, add to the sauce and stir over a gentle heat for 5 minutes.

Place the veal and the onions in a casserole dish and pour the sauce over the top. Simmer over a low heat, season to taste with salt, lemon juice and pepper and garnish with parsley.

Borscht with beef

Prep and cook time: 3 hours
Cannot be frozen
Serves: 4

Ingredients:
1500 ml | 6 cups beef stock
750 g | 2 lbs braising steak
1 tsp salt
1 tsp peppercorns
1 tsp juniper berries
1 bay leaf
200 g | ½ lb celeriac|celery root, grated
500 g | 1 ¼ lbs red beets, chopped
2 onions, diced
1 garlic clove, chopped
1 tbsp butter
3 tbsp wine vinegar
¼ tsp sugar
400 g | 2 cups chopped tomatoes
250 g | ½ lb white cabbage
1 sprig dill
2 tbsp soured cream

Method:

Put the beef, salt, peppercorns, juniper berries and bay leaf in a large pot with the beef stock and bring to a boil.
Simmer for 1 ½ hours.

Take the meat from the pot. Remove any fat and sinews and cut into bite-sized pieces. Strain the liquid.

Heat the oil in a large pot. Sauté the onions and garlic for approximately 3 minutes until they begin to brown.
Add the celeriac/celery root and beets. Continue cooking for an additional 3 minutes.

Pour in enough of the beef stock to cover the vegetables. Add the vinegar, sugar and pepper and simmer over a low light for 30 minutes.

Finely chop the cabbage or slice into thin strips.

Add the tomatoes and cabbage to the other vegetables. Add enough beef stock to cover and simmer for an additional 30 minutes.

Rinse the dill and shake off any excess moisture. Chop finely.

Stir the cubed beef into the borscht.

Season to taste with vinegar, sugar and salt and stir in the dill.

Serve with the soured cream as a garnish.

Sausage and bean stew

Prep and cook time: 50 minutes
Can be frozen
Serves: 4

Ingredients:
500 g | 1 ¼ lbs waxy potatoes, cubed
400 g | 1 lb green|string beans, halved
1 onion, diced
1 tbsp butter
1 bay leaf
1 garlic clove, crushed
1 tbsp tomato paste
2 tbsp flour
750 ml | 3 cups vegetable stock
300 g | ¾ pound frankfurter sausages
white wine vinegar

Method:

Sauté the onion in hot butter. Stir in the tomato paste, add the flour and continue to sauté briefly.

Pour in the stock and add the potatoes, bay leaf and crushed garlic clove. Simmer gently for approximately 30 minutes. After 10 minutes, add the green/string beans.

Slice the sausages in bite-sized pieces, add them to the stew and continue to cook for a further 5 minutes.

Season the stew with the salt, pepper and vinegar and allow the stew to rest for a few minutes before serving.

Chicken and vegetable stew

Prep and cook time: 1 hour 20 minutes
Cannot be frozen
Serves: 4

Ingredients:
2 large spring onions|scallions
400 g | 1 lb floury potatoes
2 carrots
2 small parsnips or parsley roots
1 chicken, jointed
2 tbsp olive oil
2 cloves garlic, peeled
300 ml | 1 ⅓ cups chicken stock
1 bay leaf
1 tsp fresh thyme leaves
4 sage leaves

Method:
Wash and trim the spring onions/scallions and cut into
5 cm / 2" lengths. Peel the potatoes and dice.

Peel the carrots and parsnips and quarter lengthwise.

Season the chicken pieces with salt and pepper. Heat the oil
in a large pan and brown the chicken pieces on all sides.

Add the vegetables, garlic, bay leaf and stock.
Cover and stew gently for about 1 hour. Stir frequently
and add more stock if necessary.

Add the thyme and sage leaves to the stew. Cook for 5 more
minutes, check the seasoning and serve.

Bean soup with bacon, rosemary and garlic

Prep and cook time: 1 hour Soak: 12 hours
Can be frozen
Serves: 4

Ingredients:
250 g | 1 ¾ cups dried haricot beans
1 bay leaf
½ tsp black peppercorns
2 onions, chopped
300 g | ¾ lb waxy potatoes, peeled and diced
2 carrots, diced
2 cloves garlic, chopped
2 tbsp butter
150 g | 6 oz green|string beans
200 g | 1 cup chopped bacon
apple vinegar

Method:

Soak the dried beans overnight in water.

Rinse the beans, put in a large pan and cover with fresh water.

Add the pepper corns and bay leaf to the pan, bring to a boil, turn down the heat and allow to simmer gently for 45 minutes.

Remove the stem and tip from the green/string beans and slice in half.

Sauté the potatoes, carrots, onion, bacon and garlic in hot butter for 10 minutes and then add them to the soup.

Simmer for 10 minutes and then add the beans.

Continue cooking until the vegetables are tender and can be easily pierced with a fork.

Season the stew with salt, pepper and vinegar to taste and serve.

casseroles.

Braised beef with vegetables

Prep and cook time: 3 hours
Cannot be frozen
Serves: 4

Ingredients:
2 bulbs fennel, sliced
2 stalks celery, sliced
2 onions, chopped
2 carrots, chopped
1 parsnip, chopped
1 kg | 2 ¼ lbs braising beef,
boned and rolled
4 tbsp sunflower oil
50 g | 2 slices bacon, diced
1 tsp allspice berries, crushed
1 tsp peppercorns, crushed
2 bay leaves
500 ml | 2 cups beef stock

Method:

Wash the beef, pat dry and season all over with salt and pepper.

Heat the oil in a large ovenproof pot. Brown the beef in hot oil on all sides, remove and set aside.

Fry the bacon in the remaining oil, add the onion and the vegetables and sauté until browned.

Add the crushed allspice, peppercorns and bay leaves and pour in about half the beef stock. Put the beef on top of the vegetables, cover and braise for about 2 - 2 ½ hours over a low heat until the meat is tender. Add the remaining beef stock gradually during cooking and turn the beef every so often.

Season to taste with salt and pepper and serve.

Sweet potato bake with crabmeat

Prep and cook time: 1 hour 15 minutes
Can be frozen
Serves: 4

Ingredients:
200 g | 2 cups crabmeat
2 onions, chopped
2 cloves garlic, chopped
50 g | ¼ cup butter
¼ tsp allspice, ground
1 kg | 2 ¼ pounds sweet potatoes
100 ml | 7 tbsp milk
200 ml | ⅞ cup coconut milk
200 g | 1 cup crème fraiche
Tabasco
50 g | ⅔ cup grated coconut

Method:
Heat oven to 180°C (160°C fan) 375°F, gas 5.

Carefully wash the crabmeat and leave to drain.

Heat about half the butter in a skillet and cook the onions and garlic until translucent.

Add the crabmeat, season with salt, pepper and allspice and remove from the heat.

Peel the sweet potatoes and slice very finely, using a mandolin if available.

Butter a baking dish with the rest of the butter and cover the base with half of the sliced sweet potatoes. Cover with the crabmeat and finish off with the rest of the sliced potatoes.

Mix the milk, coconut milk and crème fraiche in a pan, bring to the boil briefly and remove from the heat. Season well with salt and pepper, add Tabasco to taste and pour over the sweet potato bake.

Sprinkle with grated coconut and bake in the preheated oven for 45 minutes until golden brown. Serve immediately.

Rabbit stifado

Prep and cook time: 1 hour 30 minutes
Can be frozen
Serves: 4

Ingredients:
1 prepared rabbit, approx. 1.5 kg | 3 lbs
4 tbsp olive oil
2 stalks celery, chopped
2 carrots, chopped
2 parsnips, chopped
150 g | 1 ½ cups pearl onions, peeled
2 onions, chopped
2 cloves garlic, chopped
2 tbsp tomato paste
2 slices bacon
500 ml | 2 cups dry white wine
2 allspice berries
5 peppercorns
5 coriander seeds
2 fresh bay leaves
½ tbsp thyme leaves

Method:

Heat 2 tbsp of the oil in a large pan, brown the rabbit portions on all sides and remove from the pan.

Add the remaining oil, add the vegetables and cook for 5 minutes. Season with salt and pepper, stir in the tomato paste and the white wine.

Grind the allspice, pepper, coriander, bay leaves and thyme in a mortar and pestle, add to the vegetables and bring briefly to a boil.

Place the rabbit portions back into the pan and simmer over a low heat for around 1 hour.

Season with salt and pepper and serve.

Braised beef roulades

Prep and cook time: 1 hour 40 minutes
Can be frozen
Serves: 4

Ingredients:
600 g | 1 ½ lbs flank steak, cut
into 4 and lightly pounded
1 tbsp hot mustard
8 small pickled gherkins,
sliced into sticks
4 slices smoked bacon
1 tbsp plain|all purpose flour
2 tbsp vegetable oil
1 tbsp paprika
1 tbsp tomato paste
200 ml | ⅞ cup dry red wine
400 ml | 1 ⅔ cups beef stock
2 carrots, finely chopped
3 shallots, sliced
2 tbsp capers

Method:
Heat the oven to 160°C (140°C fan) 325°F, gas 3.

Spread each piece of beef with mustard, lay over 1 slice bacon and a few gherkins, roll each one tightly and tie with kitchen string.

Dust the roulades with flour. Heat the oil in an ovenproof pan and brown the roulades on all sides.

Stir in the paprika and tomato paste, pour on the wine and stock and bring to a boil, stirring gently.

Add the carrots and shallots to the meat and cook in the oven for 60-70 minutes, turning the roulades frequently.

Add the capers and season the sauce with salt and pepper. Remove the string before serving.

Porcini al forno

Prep and cook time: 1 hour
Cannot be frozen
Serves: 4

Ingredients:
750 g | 1 ½ lbs potatoes, peeled
500 g | 1 lb porcini mushrooms,
finely sliced
2 cloves garlic, chopped
40 g | 2 cups fresh parsley, chopped
4 g of oregano, chopped
4 tbsp olive oil
freshly grated nutmeg
1 tbsp lemon juice
250 ml | 1 cup chicken stock
60 g | ½ cup Pecorino cheese,
freshly grated

Method:
Heat the oven to 200°C (180°C fan) 400°F, gas 6.

Boil the potatoes for 20 minutes until done.

Fry the mushrooms in 2 tbsp of oil. Add the garlic and herbs reserving 1-2 tbsp of herbs to garnish. Fry for a further 3-4 minutes. Season with salt, pepper, nutmeg and lemon juice.

Grease an oven-proof dish with the remaining oil.

Drain the potatoes, chop into slices and layer up in the dish with the mushroom mixture.

Pour over the stock and scatter with Pecorino.

Bake for 20 minutes until golden brown and serve scattered with the reserved herbs.

Venison with grapes, bacon and croutons

Prep and cook time: 3 hours Marinate: 12 hours
Cannot be frozen
Serves: 4

Ingredients:

For the ragout:
800 g | 2 pounds venison, (shoulder or neck), chopped chunks
4 sprigs thyme
2 tbsp red wine vinegar
500 ml | 2 cups dry red wine
4 allspice berries
1 tsp peppercorns
6 juniper berries
1 bay leaf
2 tbsp oil
2 onions, chopped
2 carrots, chopped
2 stalks celery, chopped
1 clove garlic, chopped
1 tbsp tomato paste
200 ml | 7/8 cup beef stock
150 g | 1 1/2 cups white seedless grapes, peeled
1 tbsp butter
100 g | 1/2 cup bacon, sliced into strips
1 - 2 tbsp cranberry jelly

For the croutons:
2 slices bread, crusts removed, cut into triangles
2 tbsp butter

For the potato noodles:
600 g | 1 1/2 pounds floury potatoes
1 egg
100 g | 1/2 cup plain|all purpose flour
nutmeg
3 tbsp butter
2 tbsp ground hazelnuts (cob nuts)

Method:

Place the venison in a bowl with the thyme.
Pour over the vinegar and wine cover and marinate overnight.

Take the meat out and sieve the marinade.
Place the allspice berries, peppercorns, juniper berries and bay leaf in a herb bag and tie it tightly.

Heat the oil in a pan and fry the meat. Add the vegetables, fry until they are slightly browned and stir in the tomato paste. Pour in the marinade and let it reduce. Cover and simmer gently for 1 hour. Add the beef stock and the herb bag and simmer for a further 30 minutes, stirring occasionally.

Place the grapes in a small pan with the butter.
Fry the bacon in a non-stick pan without oil for 2-3 minutes.

For the croutons, heat the butter in a pan and fry the bread triangles until golden brown.

For the potato noodles, steam the potatoes for 30 minutes until done. Peel, mash and let cool. Add the egg and enough flour to make a smooth, soft dough; it should not be sticky. Season with salt and nutmeg. With floured hands, make dough rolls.

Boil the potato noodles and simmer for 2-3 minutes until they float to the top; dip into cold water and drain.

Take the meat out of the sauce. Remove the herb bag and sieve the sauce. Return the meat to the sauce and season with salt, pepper and cranberry jelly.

Fry the grapes gently. Heat the butter and hazelnuts in a pan and heat the potato noodles.

Serve on plates. Sprinkle with the bacon and grapes and serve with the croutons and potato noodles.

Chicken tagine with olives and salted lemons

Prep and cook time: 1 hour 40 minutes
Can be frozen
Serves: 4

Ingredients:
1 chicken
1 onion, chopped
1 ½ salted lemons
50 g | ¼ cup butter
2 tbsp olive oil
3 cloves garlic, crushed
1 tsp ground ginger
8 threads saffron
600 g | 1 ½ lbs potatoes,
peeled and sliced
125 g | 1 ¼ cups green olives, pitted
2 tbsp fresh coriander|cilantro,
chopped
2 tbsp parsley, chopped

To garnish:
parsley leaves

Method:
Rub the chicken inside and out with salt and pepper and set aside.

Remove the flesh and seeds from the salted lemons. Rinse the rind and pat dry, then chop roughly and set aside.

Heat the butter and oil in a flameproof roasting dish, add the onions and garlic and cook until translucent.

Add the ginger, saffron and 2 cups water and mix well. Season with salt and pepper.

Add the chicken and turn several times, until it is coated in sauce on all sides. Bring to the boil, add the potatoes, cover and simmer gently for 45 minutes, turning the chicken frequently so that it absorbs the sauce evenly. Add a little more hot water during cooking if necessary.

Stir in the olives, lemons, coriander/cilantro and parsley, cover and simmer for a further 20-25 minutes. Season to taste.

When the chicken is cooked, take it out, cover and keep warm. If the sauce is too thin, boil over a high heat to reduce it slightly.

Carve the chicken and arrange on a warmed platter (tagine). Top with olives and pieces of lemon rind and pour the sauce over. Put the lid on the tagine and serve immediately.

Fish and seafood cobbler

Prep and cook time: 1 hour 30 minutes
Cannot be frozen
Serves: 4

Ingredients:
2 tbsp oil
2 shallots, chopped
1 clove garlic, chopped
100 g | 1 ½ cups mushrooms chopped
1 courgette|zucchini, chopped
2 tomatoes, finely chopped
100 ml | 7 tbsp white wine
200 ml | ⅞ cup fish stock
1 - 2 tbsp cornflour|cornstarch
2 tbsp parsley, chopped
500 g | 1 lb fish fillets
150 g | 1 ½ cups prawns|shrimps, prepared
250 g | 2 cups plain|all purpose flour
3 tsp baking powder
½ tsp salt
150 ml | ⅔ cup milk
75 g | ¾ cup cheese, grated
Flour for the work surface

Method:
Heat the oven to 200°C (180°C fan) 400°F, gas 6.

Heat the oil in a pan and soften the shallots and garlic. Add the mushrooms, courgette/zucchini and tomatoes.

Pour in the white wine and fish stock and bring to a boil. Mix the cornflour/cornstarch to a paste with cold water and stir in to bind the sauce.

Remove from the heat and stir in the parsley, fish and prawns/shrimps; season with salt and pepper and turn into an ovenproof dish.

To make the topping, mix together the flour, baking powder, salt, butter and just enough milk to make a smooth dough which does not stick to your hands.

Roll out to about 1.5 cm / ½" thick on a floured work surface and cut out circles of about 3 cm / 1 ¼" diameter. Brush the circles with milk and lay on top of the fish mixture, overlapping like tiles.

Scatter with cheese and bake for 30 minutes until golden brown.

Sausage hotpot

Prep and cook time: 45 minutes
Cannot be frozen
Serves: 4

Ingredients:
800 g | 2 lbs small pork sausages
1 tbsp olive oil
400 g | ½ pound shallots, quartered
1 clove garlic, finely chopped
1 tbsp sugar
2 tbsp balsamic vinegar
125 ml | ½ cup chicken stock
600 g | 1 ½ lbs potatoes, thinly sliced
2 tbsp butter

Method:
Heat the oven to 220°C (200°C fan) 425°F, gas 7.

Fry the sausages with 1 tsp of oil in a skillet until golden brown and remove from the heat.

Heat the remaining oil in an ovenproof pan and cook the onions and garlic until translucent.

Sprinkle in the sugar and allow to caramelize slightly, deglaze with the vinegar, reduce a little and then pour in the stock.

Add the sausages to the shallots, season with salt and pepper and lay the potato slices on top. Cover with a lid and cook for 5 minutes.

Remove the lid, put butter in small pieces on the potatoes and bake in the oven for around 15 minutes until browned.

Cassoulet with pork and duck

Prep and cook time: 2 hours 45 minutes
Cannot be frozen
Serves: 4

Ingredients:
4 duck legs
400 g | 1 lb belly pork, diced
1 large onion, chopped
150 g | ¾ lb chorizo, sliced
4 cloves garlic, finely chopped
2 tbsp flour
300 ml | 1 ⅓ cups dry red wine
300 ml | 1 ⅓ cups chicken stock
400 g | 2 cups chopped tomatoes
600 g | 2 ½ cups haricot beans
1 tsp freshly chopped rosemary
1 tsp freshly chopped thyme
1 bay leaf
3 tbsp breadcrumbs
2 tbsp freshly grated Parmesan

for the garlic bread:
4 cloves garlic, crushed
4 tbsp olive oil
4 tbsp finely chopped parsley
1 small French stick

Method:
Heat the oven to 180°C (160°C fan) 375°F, gas 5.

Heat a large skillet without oil and brown the duck pieces all over for about 5 minutes. Transfer to an ovenproof pot.

Using the same skillet fry the pork and the onion together for about 5 minutes, until the meat is browned on all sides.
Add the chorizo and garlic and fry for a further 3 minutes or so.

Dust with flour and stir until the flour has all been absorbed by the frying juices. Gradually stir in the wine and the chicken stock. Add the tomatoes, season well with pepper and bring to the boil briefly.

Add the beans, rosemary, thyme and bay leaf to the duck in the pot. Then add the contents of the skillet and mix well.
Press down with a fork so that all the ingredients are in the liquid.

Scatter with breadcrumbs and Parmesan. Cover with a lid and cook in the preheated oven for about 1 ½ hours. Then remove the lid and bake for a further 30 minutes, until golden brown.

For the garlic bread, split the French stick lengthwise and toast under a hot broiler (grill). Mix the garlic and parsley with the oil and season with salt and pepper. Brush over the cut side over the toasted bread.

Alsacian bake

Prep and cook time: 3 hours Marinate: 24 hours
Can be frozen
Serves: 4

Ingredients:

250 g | ½ lb pork neck,
chopped into chunks

250 g | ½ lb mutton,
chopped into chunks

250 g | ½ lb beef brisket,
chopped into chunks

4 shallots, sliced into rings

2 cloves garlic, finely chopped

20 g | 1 cup parsley, leaves

4 g thyme, leaves

2 bay leaves

500 ml | 2 cups dry white wine

200 g | 2 cups onions, sliced

600 g | 1 ½ lbs waxy potatoes, sliced

Method:

Place the meat with the shallots, garlic, herbs, bay leaves and wine in a bowl. Cover and marinate in the refrigerator for 24 hours.

Heat the oven to 200°C (180°C fan) 400°F, gas 6.

Layer the meat, onions and potatoes in an oven-proof dish.
Season each layer with salt and pepper.
Top with a final layer of potatoes and pour on the marinade.

Put the lid on tightly and cook for 2 - 2 ½ hours.
Check the seasoning and serve.

Moussaka

Prep and cook time: 1 hour 45 minutes
Can be frozen
Serves: 4

Ingredients:
2 medium aubergines|eggplants
olive oil
200 g | 1 ¼ cups onions, chopped
600 g | 3 cups chopped tomatoes
600 g | 1 ½ lb ground beef or lamb
250 ml | 1 cup dry white wine
2 ½ cm sugar
½ tsp cinnamon
1 tsp dried oregano
25 g | 1 cup parsley, chopped
4 tbsp sunflower seeds
100 g | 2 cups breadcrumbs
100 g | 1 cup Gruyère cheese, grated
40 g | 2 tbsp butter
4 tbsp flour
750 ml | 3 cups milk
nutmeg, freshly grated
2 tsp lemon juice
3 eggs
200 g | 2 cups feta cheese

Method:
Heat the oven to 180°C (160°C fan) 375°F, gas 5.

Wash the aubergines/eggplants and slice lengthwise into slices approximately ½ cm / ¼" thick. Lay in salted water for about 20 minutes, then drain and pat dry.

Heat 3 – 4 tbsp olive oil in a large non-stick frying pan and fry the eggplant in batches over a medium heat until lightly browned. Add more oil as necessary. Drain on paper towels.

Heat 3 tbsp oil in a frying pan and cook the onions until translucent. Stir in the meat and fry over a high heat, breaking it up to brown right through.

Stir in the tomatoes, white wine, salt, sugar, cinnamon and pepper, cover and cook over a medium heat for about 5 minutes. Stir the parsley, sunflower seeds and oregano into the meat. Cook for a further 5 minutes, then let cool.
Mix the breadcrumbs (keeping back 2 tbsp) and half of the Gruyère cheese into the meat. Stir 1 egg into the meat.

Heat the butter in a saucepan, stir in the flour and cook for 2 minutes. Slowly stir in the milk and bring to a boil.

Cook over a low heat, stirring, for at least 5 minutes, then season to taste with salt, pepper, nutmeg and lemon juice. Let cool slightly. Beat 2 eggs and stir into the white sauce with the rest of the Gruyère cheese.

Butter a baking dish and sprinkle with the rest of the breadcrumbs.

Line the dish with half of the aubergine/eggplant slices, add the meat and top with the rest of the aubergine/eggplant .

Cover with the sauce. Crumble the feta cheese over the moussaka and bake in the preheated oven for about 1 hour.

Cod casserole with chilli and lemon

Prep and cook time: 1 hour 20 minutes
Cannot be frozen
Serves: 4

Ingredients:
800 g | 2 lbs cod fillet, divided
into portions
1 lemon, peeled and thinly sliced
2 cloves garlic, peeled and thinly sliced
3 tbsp olive oil
2 red chilli peppers, deseeded
125 ml | ½ cup fish stock
3 eggs

To garnish:
fresh dill

Method:
Heat the oven to 180°C (160°C fan) 350°F, gas 4.

Lay the fish fillets in an oven-proof dish with the lemon and garlic slices. Drizzle with olive oil and season with salt and pepper.

Chop one chilli pepper into fine strips and puree the other with the fish stock and eggs. Season well with salt and pepper and pour the mixture over the fish.

Bake for 45 minutes.

Scatter with dill and chilli strips to serve.

Vegetable bake

Prep and cook time: 1 hour
Can be frozen
Serves: 4

Ingredients:
1 clove garlic
butter, for the dish
400 g | 1 lb potatoes
200g | ½ lb sweet potaoes
2 carrots
200 ml | ⅞ cup cream
1 tsp fresh thyme leaves
50 g | ½ cup Emmental cheese, grated
2 tbsp crème fraiche
nutmeg, freshly grated

Method:

Heat oven to 200°C (180°C fan) 400°F, gas 6.

Peel the garlic. Rub the baking dish with the garlic clove and then butter the dish.

Wash and peel the potatoes and slice very thinly, using a mandolin vegetable slicer if available. Peel the carrots and slice very thinly at an angle. Fill the baking dish with alternate layers of potato, sweet potato and carrot slices, finishing with a layer of potatoes.

Mix together the cream, thyme, cheese and crème fraiche and season with salt, pepper and nutmeg.
Pour over the vegetables; the potatoes should be just covered. Add a little more cream if necessary.

Bake in the preheated oven for about 35 minutes until the top is nicely browned and the vegetables are tender.

home
cooking.

Grilled spare ribs with rosemary

Prep and cook time: 35 minutes Marinating time: 2 hours
Can be frozen
Serves: 4

Ingredients:
2000 g | 4 ½ lbs pork ribs
3 garlic cloves, crushed
125 ml | ½ cup olive oil
4 - 5 fresh rosemary sprigs

Method:

Separate the spare ribs into individual pieces (3-4 ribs).

Mix the garlic and with olive oil, salt and pepper for the marinade. Mix the ribs with the marinade and lay the rosemary sprigs on the meat. Leave to marinade for at least 2 hours, overnight for the best results.

Grill the ribs slowly for 25 minutes, turning and brushing with the marinade every now and then, using the rosemary sprigs like a brush.

Beef cheeks with potato dumplings

Prep and cook time: 3 hours 15 minutes
Can be frozen
Serves: 4

Ingredients:
800 g | 2 lbs beef cheeks
1 onion, chopped
2 carrots, chopped
200 g | ½ lb celeriac|celery root, chopped
2 tbsp sunflower oil
2 tbsp tomato paste
250 ml | 1 cup dry red wine
250 g beef stock
4 juniper berries
1 tsp pepper corns
1 bay leaf
2 allspice seeds
1 bulb fennel
1 tbsp butter
100 ml | 7 tbsp dry white wine

For the potato dumplings:
1 kg | 2 ¼ lbs floury potatoes, washed and peeled
1 kg | 1 cup flour
1 egg
salt
2 tbsp cornflour|cornstarch

Method:

Heat 1 tbsp oil in a large pan, brown the cheeks on all sides and set aside.

Add the remaining oil to the pan and fry the onions, carrots and celeriac/celery root for 5 minutes. Stir in the tomato paste and deglaze the pan with half of the red wine. Reduce the liquid slightly.

Pour in the remaining wine and the beef stock. Put in the cheeks, juniper berries, pepper corns, bay leaf and allspice seeds in the pan. Cover and allow to simmer gently for approximately 2 ½ hours, turning the cheeks frequently.

For the dumplings, boil the potatoes in salted water for approximately 30 minutes until tender. Drain and mash the potatoes, adding the flour, eggs and salt, and mix into a dough.

Bring a pot of well salted water to a boil. Dissolve the cornflour/cornstarch in some cold water. Pour it in the boiling water.

Using damp hands, make round balls/dumplings out of the potato dough and put them in the boiling water.
Allow the dumplings to boil for approximately 20 minutes.

Clean and wash the fennel. Cut into strips. Sauté in hot butter. Deglaze the pan with the white wine. Cover and allow to simmer gently for approximately 10 minutes.

Remove the cheeks from the sauce. Reduce the sauce a little if desired. Strain and season with salt and pepper to taste.
Slice the cheeks and put them back in the sauce.
Allow the slices to soak a little.

Put the cheek slices and dumplings on the plates and pour the sauce on top. Garnish with the fennel strips.

Pork fillet with mushroom stuffing in puff pastry

Prep and cook time: 1 hour 15 minutes
Cannot be frozen
Serves: 4

Ingredients:
300 g | ¾ lb puff pastry
4 shallots, finely chopped
2 garlic cloves, finely chopped
250 g | 2 cups mushrooms, finely chopped
2 tbsp butter
2 tbsp dry white wine
800 g | 2 lbs pork fillet
2 tbsp vegetable oil
250 g | ¼ lb ground pork
2 tbsp bread crumbs
1 tsp fresh chopped thyme
2 egg yolks

Method:
Preheat the oven to 200°C (180°C fan) 400°F, gas 6.

Heat the butter in a skillet and fry the shallots and garlic, then add the mushrooms. Cook until all the moisture has evaporated.

Add the white wine, remove the pan from the heat and allow to cool.

Wash the meat, pat dry. Sprinkle both sides with salt and pepper. Heat the oil in a separate pan and sear all sides until well browned. Remove the meat from the pan.

Combine the mushrooms with the ground pork, bread crumbs and thyme and mix well. Season with salt and pepper.

Roll out the puff pastry so that it is large enough to accommodate the filling.

Spread approximately one quarter of the ground pork/mushroom mixture in the middle of the pastry. Put the meat on top. Spread the rest of the ground pork/mushroom mixture around it and cover with the pastry.

Wrap it tightly and pinch the edges well to form a tight seam.

With the seam facing downwards place it on a greased cookie sheet. Brush with the egg yolks and bake in the oven for approximately 45 minutes. Brush with egg yolk again roughly 10 minutes before the end of the cooking time.

Slice and serve.

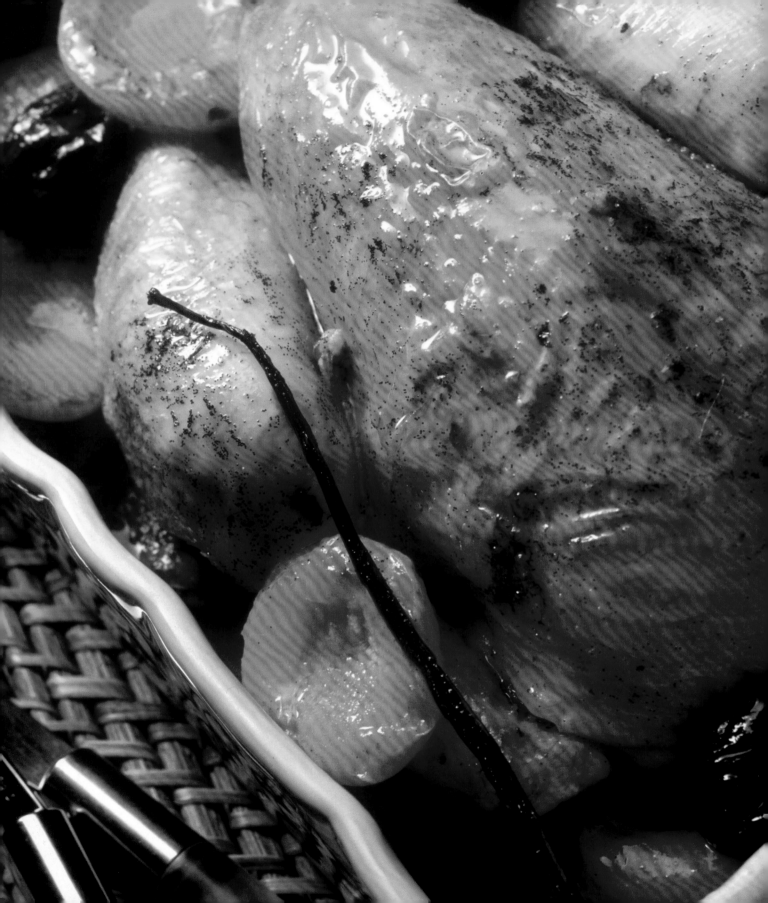

Stewed and roasted chicken with apricot stuffing

Prep and cook time: 1 hour 30 minutes
Can be frozen
Serves: 4

Ingredients:
400 g | 1 lb plums
400 g | 1 lb apricots
2 tbsp lemon juice
freshly ground pepper
1 tsp ground cloves
1 small chicken
250 ml | 1 cup chicken stock
4 tbsp apple jelly
1 vanilla pod
1 tbsp apple juice

Method:
Preheat the oven to 200°C (180°C fan) 400°F, gas 6.

Wash and de-stone the plums and apricots. Slice in half. Mix them with the lemon juice, pepper and cloves and stuff the mixture inside the chicken, reserving a few.

Truss the chicken using wooden skewers. Place the chicken in a deep ovenproof dish and pour over the stock. Arrange the fruit around the chicken, cover, place in the preheated oven and allow to stew for approximately 45 minutes.

Open the vanilla pod and scrape out the seeds.
Mix them with the apple juice and jelly and baste the chicken with the mixture.

Put the vanilla pod in with the chicken, remove the lid and roast for a further 15 minutes.

Arrange the chicken, sauce and fruit on a serving platter.

Boeuf bourguignon

Prep and cook time: 2 hours
Cannot be frozen
Serves: 4

Ingredients:
800 g | 2 lbs braising beef, cubed
2 carrots, cut into bite size pieces
2 stalks celery, chopped
300 g | 2 cups brown button mushrooms, halved
400 g | 1 pound shallots, halved
2 cloves garlic, chopped
6 tbsp olive oil
500 ml | 2 cups robust red wine
2 bay leaves
3 - 4 sprigs rosemary
100 g | 4 slices bacon, diced
1000 ml | 4 cups beef stock

Method:

Heat 4 tbsp oil in a large pan and brown the meat, in batches if necessary, then set aside.

Add the shallots and garlic to the pan and fry until they're beginning to soften. Deglaze with the red wine and cook until reduced by half.

Return the meat to the pan then add the bay leaves and stock and cook over a low heat for 1 $\frac{1}{2}$ hours.

20 minutes before the end of cooking time add the carrots and celery.

Strip the leaves from the rosemary stalks and chop finely.

Fry the bacon in the remaining oil, add the mushrooms and cook for 5 minutes.

Mix into the beef, cook for another 5 minutes and sprinkle with rosemary before serving.

Cannelloni with mixed vegetable sauce

Prep and cook time: 1 hour 30 minutes
Can be frozen
Serves: 4

Ingredients:
2 onions, chopped
2 cloves garlic, chopped
1 yellow bell pepper, diced
1 small courgette|zucchini, diced
1 small fennel bulb, diced
1 stale bread roll
2 tbsp olive oil
800 g | 3 ½ cups chopped tomatoes
2 tsp dried oregano
250 g | 2 ½ cups mozzarella, sliced
300 g | 1 ½ cups ground beef
300 g | 1 ½ cups ground pork
1 egg
250 g | ½ lb dried cannelloni tubes
butter, for the dish

Method:
Heat the oven to 200°C (180°C fan) 400°F, gas 6.

Soak the bread roll in water.

Heat the oil in a pan and cook half of the garlic and onion with the fennel until translucent.

Add the tomatoes with their juice and 1 tsp oregano.
Bring to the boil and simmer over a low heat for 15 minutes, until reduced slightly. Add the bell peppers and courgette/zucchini after 10 minutes and season with salt and pepper.

Mix the pork and beef with the remaining onion, garlic and oregano, add the egg and squeezed-out bread roll.
Season with salt and pepper.

Fill the cannelloni tubes with the meat mixture, place in a greased baking dish and pour over the tomato sauce.

Top with mozzarella slices and bake in the preheated oven for about 35 minutes.

Duck confit

Prep and cook time: 3 hours 30 minutes Marinating time: 12 hours
Cannot be frozen
Serves: 4

Ingredients:
4 duck legs
200 g | 1 cup sea salt
2 tsp black peppercorns,
slightly crushed
2 sprigs rosemary
3 tbsp honey
500 g | 4 cups shallots
1 kg | 5 cups duck or goose fat
4 slices bread, to serve

Method:
Wash and dry the duck legs. Cut through the sinews to the bone below the calf on each leg, so that the meat can contract during cooking.

Pick the leaves from the rosemary stalks and mix the leaves with the honey, pepper and salt. Rub the mixture into the duck legs, cover and leave to marinade overnight.

Heat oven to 150°C (130°C fan) 300°F, gas 2.

Heat a little duck fat in an ovenproof dish and brown the duck legs all over. Remove the duck then add the whole shallots and cook briefly until slightly browned.

Return the meat to the pan, add the rest of the duck fat, so that the meat is covered. Put the pan in the bottom of the oven for about 3 hours, until the meat is tender and nicely browned.

To serve, toast the bread and put on plates. Put a piece of duck on each slice of bread, add a few of shallots and serve.

Roasted lamb in a salt crust

Prep and cook time: 2 hours
Cannot be frozen
Serves: 4

Ingredients:
1 kg | 2 ¼ lbs boned lamb
2 sprigs rosemary
8 sprigs thyme
2 tbsp olive oil
freshly ground pepper
2 kg | 4 ½ lbs sea salt
4 egg whites

Method:

Preheat the oven to 160°C (140°C fan) 325°F, gas 3.

Strip leaves from the rosemary and thyme stems. Chop finely.

Mix half of the herbs with the olive oil and a little pepper. Rub the meat well with the paste.

Mix the sea salt with the remaining herbs and egg whites (and a little water if necessary) to form a soft, but not sticky, paste.

Put approximately one third of the salt/egg paste in a roasting pan lined with parchment paper. Put the meat on top.

Encase the meat completely with the remaining salt mixture. Bake in the preheated oven for approximately 1 ½ hours.

At the end of the baking time, take the meat out of the oven and allow rest for 15 minutes. Break open the crust and serve the meat.

Steak and kidney pudding

Prep and cook time: 2 hours 30 minutes
Cannot be frozen
Serves: 4

Ingredients:
For the pastry:
300 g | 2 ½ cups plain|all purpose flour
2 ½ cm salt
150 g | 3/4 cup butter
2 eggs

For the filling:
200 g | ½ lb ox kidney
600 g | 1 ½ lbs rump steak
2 tbsp flour
1 large onion, chopped
2 carrots, sliced
4 tbsp oil
2 tsp Worcester sauce
125 ml | ½ cup dry red wine
100 ml | 7 tbsp beef stock

Method:
Heat oven to 200°C (180°C fan) 400°F, gas 6.

Put the flour in a heap on the work surface, mix in the salt and make a well in the centre of the flour. Cut the butter into small pieces and scatter around the well.

Break the eggs into the middle and chop all ingredients with a knife until they have the consistency of breadcrumbs.
Quickly knead to a dough using your hands, form into a ball, wrap in plastic wrap and chill for 30 minutes.

Cut the kidney open lengthwise, wash and remove the white core. Soak in cold water for about 45 minutes. Cut the beef into approximately 1.5 cm / ¾" cubes and dust with 1 tbsp flour. Heat 3 tbsp oil in a pan and brown the meat on all sides over a high heat, a few pieces at a time. Take out of the pan and set aside.

Fry the onion in the pan until translucent and season with salt, pepper and Worcester sauce. Return the meat to the pan and add the carrots, red wine and stock, stirring well.
Bring to the boil, cover and simmer for 5 minutes.

Drain the kidney halves, wash again and dab dry.
Cut into approximately 1.5 cm / ¾" cubes, dust with the remaining flour and fry on all sides in the rest of the oil for 2 - 3 minutes. Season with salt and pepper. Add the kidneys to the meat pan and remove from the heat

Grease 4 350 ml / 1 ½ cup capacity ovenproof bowls.

Roll the pastry out thinly between 2 layers of plastic wrap and line the bowls with about ¾ of the pastry. Fill each lined basin with meat and make lids from the rest of the pastry.
Make a small hole in the middle of each lid.

Bake in the preheated oven for about 30 minutes.
To serve turn out onto plates.

Crisp roasted pork belly

Prep and cook time: 1 hour 20 minutes
Cannot be frozen
Serves: 4

Ingredients:
1 kg | 2 ¼ lbs pork belly
100 g | ½ cup sea salt
freshly ground pepper
3 sprigs rosemary

Method:

Preheat the oven to 180°C (160°C fan) 375°F, gas 5.

Wash the pork belly and dry thoroughly with paper towels. Make crisscross incisions along the length of the skin and season liberally with salt and pepper, rubbing into the incisions.

Place two rosemary sprigs on an oven rack in a deep roasting pan and put the meat on top.

Roast for 60-70 minutes until crispy.

Garnish with the remaining rosemary sprig and serve.

Ossobuco

Prep and cook time: 2 hours 45 minutes
Can be frozen
Serves: 4

Ingredients:
4 slices shin of veal
2 tbsp plain|all purpose flour
2 tbsp olive oil
250 ml | 1 cup white wine
250 ml | 1 cup beef stock
800 g | 2 lbs beef tomatoes,
peeled, halved
6 sprigs thyme
4 tbsp butter
2 onion, sliced in rings

Method:
Season the veal slices with salt and pepper and sprinkle with flour.

Heat the oil in a large pan and brown the slices on both sides. Pour on the wine. Reduce by half and add a little stock. Cover and cook for 2 hours, adding a little more stock when necessary.

Add the tomatoes and thyme to the meat. Braise for a further 30 minutes until done.

Heat the butter and fry the onion rings gently for 10 minutes until golden brown.

Just before serving, arrange the onion rings over the veal and season everything with salt and pepper.

Game pie

Prep and cook time: 2 hours 30 minutes Setting time: 14 hours
Cannot be frozen
Makes: 1 mould

Ingredients:
For the pastry:
500 g | 4 cups plain|all purpose flour
250 g | 1 ¼ cups butter
salt
2 eggs

For the filling/pâté:
1 stale roll
700 g | 1 ¾ lbs prepared rabbit meat
175 g | ½ lb pork belly
150 g | ¼ lb rabbit liver
4 mushrooms
4 slices smoked bacon, chopped
3 shallots, chopped
2 garlic cloves, chopped
1 tsp fresh chopped thyme
50 g | ½ cup cranberries
1 egg
1 tsp ground cloves
1 tsp ground allspice
300ml | 1 ¼ cups cognac

In addition:
butter, for the mould
1 egg yolk
2 gelatine leaves
1 tbsp grape jelly
40 ml | 8 tsp white port

Method:
For the pastry, sift the flour into a bowl and make a well in middle. Put 2 tbsp of the butter, salt, egg into the well, knead swiftly into a round ball and wrap in plastic wrap.
Allow it to rest in the refrigerator for approximately two hours.

For the filling, soften the roll in lukewarm water. Squeeze out as much moisture as possible and pull apart into pieces.

Using a food processor, coarsely chop the rabbit meat, pork belly, rabbit liver and cleaned mushrooms. Mix the shallots and garlic, along with bacon, thyme, bread pieces, cranberries, egg, salt, pepper, cloves, allspice and cognac with the meat.

Preheat the oven to 160°C, (140°C fan) 325°F, gas 3.

Roll out the pastry. Cut out two ovals for the top and bottom crusts. Cut out two strips the height of the mould for the sides. Use remaining dough to make decorations for the top.

Butter the mould. Use one oval to cover the bottom. Use the strips to cover the sides. Carefully pinch the pastry seams together. Put the meat mixture inside and smooth the top. Place the remaining pastry oval on top. Carefully pinch the seams together. Make a small hole in the middle of the top crust.

Mix the egg yolk with the tablespoon of water and brush it on the pastry shell. Decorate with the pastry leaves. Brush them with the egg yolk, too.

Place in the oven for 90 minutes. Bake until golden brown. Remove from the oven and let cool.

Soften the gelatine in cold water. Shake off excess water and dissolve it in the warmed port. Add the grape jelly and allow to melt. Pour the mixture into the pastry hole. Allow the pie to sit over night.

Oven-roasted chicken and vegetables

Prep and cook time: 1 hour
Can be frozen
Serves: 4

Ingredients:
1 chicken, jointed
$\frac{1}{2}$ tsp sweet paprika
3 tbsp honey
4 tbsp lime juice
$\frac{1}{4}$ tsp Cayenne pepper
6 tbsp olive oil
10 g | $\frac{1}{2}$ cup sage leaves
400 g | 1 lb young carrots
3 small fennel bulbs, cut into wedges
2 onions, cut into wedges
2 tbsp balsamic vinegar
100 ml | 7 tbsp chicken stock

Method:
For the marinade, mix the paprika, honey, lime juice, Cayenne and 2 tbsp of the oil and season with salt and pepper. Cover the chicken pieces with the marinade and set aside.

Heat the oven to 200°C (180°C fan) 400°F, gas 6.

Wash the carrots, peel if you wish and cut off most of the tops. Put the carrots, fennel and onions into a roasting pan with the remaining oil, turn to coat with the oil and sprinkle lightly with salt.

Drizzle with vinegar and put the chicken pieces on top. Brush the chicken on all sides with the marinade and scatter with sage leaves.

Put into the oven and roast for 35 minutes. Brush with a little more marinade after 10 minutes.

10-15 minutes before the end of cooking time pour the stock into the roasting pan (enough to cover the bottom of the dish) and continue cooking until done. Serve hot.

Potato and apple gratin

Prep and cook time: 25 minutes Baking time: 45 minutes
Can be frozen
Serves: 4

Ingredients:
butter, for the dish
2 kg | 4 ¹/₂ lbs firm-cooking potatoes
3 medium-sized cooking apples
2 tbsp lemon juice
salt & pepper
2 tsp fresh thyme, chopped
250 ml | 1 cup cream
150 g | 1 ¹/₂ cups Brie
2 tbsp butter

Method:
Butter a large gratin dish. Preheat the oven to 200°C (180°C fan) 375°F, gas 5.

Wash and peel the potatoes and slice very thinly.
Peel and quarter the apples and cut into thin wedges.
Sprinkle immediately with lemon juice to prevent browning.

Arrange the potato and apple slices in the gratin dish in alternate layers, sprinkling each layer with salt, pepper and a little thyme.

Finally pour the cream over and top with the sliced Brie.
Dot with flakes of butter and bake on the middle shelf of the oven for 45 minutes.

Serve sprinkled with fresh thyme.

Rolled pork roast with ham stuffing

Prep and cook time: 2 hours 15 minutes
Serves: 12

Ingredients:
3 kg | 6 ½ lbs pork loin, boned
5 tbsp oil
3 tbsp paprika
2 tbsp rosemary
900 ml | 4 cups chicken stock

For the stuffing:
3 onions, finely chopped
3 cloves garlic, finely chopped
1 green bell pepper, diced
400 g | 1 lb ham, diced
4 tbsp parsley, chopped
2 bay leaves, crushed

For the vegetables:
3 potatoes, cubed
3 carrots, chopped
1 aubergine|eggplant, chopped
2 bell peppers, chopped
3 onions, chopped
5 tomatoes, chopped
2 leeks, chopped
3 small courgettes|zucchinis, chopped

Method:
Preheat oven to 240°C (220°C fan) 475°F, gas 9.

Season the meat with salt and pepper.

Mix the stuffing ingredients together and spread the mixture on the meat, leaving a small border free at the edge. Roll up the meat, secure and tie with kitchen string.

Mix the oil with the paprika and rosemary and brush the meat on all sides with the mixture.

Place the meat in a large roasting pan, add the stock, cover and roast in the oven for 15 minutes. Then turn the temperature down to 180°C (160°C fan) 350°F, gas 4 and roast for about 1 ½ hours.

Remove the cover. Put the potatoes and carrots in the liquid, arrange the rest of the vegetables around the meat and continue cooking for another 30 minutes in the open roasting dish, stirring from time to time.

Spaghetti and meatballs in tomato sauce

Prep and cook time: 50 minutes
Can be frozen
Serves: 4

Ingredients:
For the sauce:
2 onions, chopped
2 garlic cloves, chopped
4 tbsp olive oil
600 g | 1 ¼ lbs chopped tomatoes
2 tbsp tomato paste
sugar

For the meatballs:
400 g | 1 lb ground beef
4 tbsp bread crumbs
1 egg
2 tbsp Parmesan cheese, grated
2 tbsp chopped herbs
(parsley, tarragon, thyme)
400 g | 14 oz spaghetti

Method:
Sauté the onions and garlic in 2 tbsp of hot oil in a saucepan. Remove half and set aside.

Stir the tomato paste into the remaining garlic and onions. Sauté together briefly. Stir in the tomatoes. Simmer, uncovered, for 30 minutes. Stir occasionally adding water if necessary.

Cook the spaghetti in salted, boiling water until al dente.

Combine the ground beef with the reserved garlic and onion, bread crumbs, egg, Parmesan cheese and herbs. Knead well. Season with salt and pepper.

With damp hands, make small meatballs with the mixture.

Sauté the meatballs in the remaining oil until brown on all sides (6 minutes). Add them to the tomato sauce and allow to sit for 2 minutes.

Season the sauce to taste with sugar, salt and pepper.
Serve the meatballs with the well drained spaghetti.

Leg of kid with garlic, carrots, potatoes and rosemary

Prep and cook time: 2 hours
Can be frozen
Serves: 4

Ingredients:
1 leg of kid, 1.2 kg | 2 ½ lbs
3 tbsp olive oil
100 ml | 7 tbsp dry white wine
1 tbsp hot mustard
4 g rosemary
4 g thyme
½ tsp caraway
200 ml | ⅞ cup chicken stock
6 baby carrots
500 g | 1 lb potatoes,
cut into thick wedges
8 cloves garlic

Method:
Heat the oven to 160°C (140°C fan) 325°F, gas 3.

Season the meat with salt and pepper. Heat the oil in a roasting pan and fry the meat on all sides. Pour in the wine.

Spread mustard on the meat, lay on the rosemary and thyme sprigs, sprinkle with caraway and pour on the stock. Cover and braise for 1 hour. Baste with the juices occasionally and add more stock if necessary.

Uncover the pan. Place the potatoes, carrots and garlic cloves around the meat and braise uncovered for a further 30 minutes. Season with salt and pepper and serve.

Cottage pie

Prep and cook time: 1 h 30 minutes
Can be frozen
Serves: 2

Ingredients:
200 g |½ lb floury potatoes, peeled
400 g | 1 lb ground beef
1 onion, chopped
1 carrot, chopped
2 stalks celery, chopped
150 ml | ⅔ cup beef stock
2 tbsp oil
1 tsp tomato paste
50 g | ½ cup cheese, grated
40 ml | 8 tsp hot milk
nutmeg
butter, to grease the dish

Method:

Heat the oven to 200°C (180°C fan) 400°F, gas 6.

Boil the potatoes for 25 minutes in salted water until done.

Fry the ground beef and vegetables in hot oil, add the tomato paste and stock and season with salt and pepper.

Drain and mash the potatoes. Stir in the hot milk and season with salt, pepper and nutmeg.

Grease a small pie dish with butter.

Turn the ground beef mixture into the dish, spread the mashed potato on top and sprinkle with cheese.

Bake in the middle of the oven for 40-45 minutes until golden brown.

Chilli con carne

Prep and cook time: 1 hour
Can be frozen
Serves: 4

Ingredients:
2 onions, chopped
3 cloves garlic, minced
1 green bell pepper, deseeded and diced
2 red chilli peppers, deseeded and finely chopped
100 g | ½ cup bacon, diced
2 tbsp vegetable oil
600 g | 1 ½ pound ground beef
1 tbsp flour
250 ml | 1 cup beef stock
400 g | 2 cups chopped tomatoes
200 g | 2 cups canned kidney beans
Cayenne pepper

To garnish:
coriander|cilantro leaves

Method:
Heat the oil in a large pan and sauté the onion and garlic until transparent.

Add the bacon, half of the chilli peppers and the bell peppers and fry briefly. Add the beef and brown well.

Sprinkle the mixture with the flour, add the tomatoes and pour the vegetable stock on top. Cook for approximately 30 minutes over low heat, stirring occasionally and adding more stock if necessary.

Drain and rinse the kidney beans and add them to the chilli. Cook for an additional 10 minutes. Season with the salt, pepper and Cayenne pepper.

Garnish with the reserved chillies and coriander/cilantro.

Roast turkey with trimmings

Prep and cook time: 3 hours 15 minutes
Cannot be frozen
Serves: 8

Ingredients:
For the stuffed turkey:
1 turkey
250 g | 1 lb ground veal
250 g | 1 lb ground pork
2 onions, chopped
25 g | 1 cup parsley
125 g | 1 ¼ cup butter
2 bread rolls
milk, for soaking
50 g | ⅓ cup ground hazelnuts
(cob nuts)
3 eggs
1 tbsp dried marjoram
½ tsp coriander seeds
½ tsp pepper corns
½ tsp caraway

For the trimmings:
1 kg | 2 ¼ lb potatoes
1 tsp fresh chopped rosemary
600 g | 1 ½ pounds sausages
4 slices bacon
800 g | 2 pounds brussel sprouts
2 tbsp cranberries, fresh or pickled

Method:
Preheat the oven to 180°C (160° fan) 350°F, gas 4.

Season the turkey with salt and pepper – inside and out.

Heat 2 tbsp of the butter and gently fry the onion.

Soften the rolls in the milk, squeeze out as much moisture as possible. Tear the rolls into pieces and sauté them briefly with the onion and then add the parsley.

When cool, mix with the ground meat, hazelnuts, eggs and spices (salt, pepper and marjoram). If necessary, add more spice to taste.

Stuff the turkey with the mixture and truss. Cover the turkey loosely with foil and place in the preheated oven (lowest rack). Roast for 2-2 ½ hours. Baste the turkey occasionally during roasting with the reserved butter.

Remove the foil 45 minutes before removing turkey from the oven.

Crush the coriander, pepper corns and caraway in a mortar. Sprinkle over the turkey.

For the trimmings:

Peel and quarter the potatoes. Mix with the rosemary and some salt.

Wrap the sausages in the bacon slices.

Wash the brussel sprouts and slice them in half.

During the last 30-40 minutes of the roasting time, place the trimmings around the turkey.

To serve, put everything on a platter and garnish with the cranberries.

Braised shoulder of lamb with fennel

Prep and cook time: 1 hour 15 minutes
Cannot be frozen
Serves: 4

Ingredients:
1 shallot, halved
1 clove garlic, crushed
1 kg | 2 lbs lamb shoulder
2 tbsp ghee
250 ml | 1 cup dry red wine
150 ml | 2/3 cup vegetable stock
1 bay leaf
6 thyme sprigs
1/4 celeriac|celery root, finely sliced
oil, for fying
2 large fennel heads
2 tbsp olive oil
3 tbsp dark soy sauce
1 tbsp honey

Method:

Remove any visible fat and sinews from the meat. Score the skin making crosswise incisions with a sharp knife and rub with salt.

Heat the ghee in a large pot, add the lamb and brown well on all sides. Place the meat with the skin facing upward in the pot; pour the wine and stock over the top.

Add the garlic, shallots, bay leaf and thyme sprigs. Cover the pot and allow to cook for 20 minutes. Turn the shoulder, adding more stock if necessary, and continue cooking for another 20 minutes.

Heat the oven to 240°C (220°C fan) 475°F, gas 9.

Meanwhile, fry the celeriac/celery root in hot oil for 3 minutes until golden brown. Allow to drain on paper towels.

Wash the fennel and cut the stalk and the bulb lengthwise into 3-4 mm pieces. Steam the chopped fennel in a pan with 50 ml of stock, shake and pat dry. Fry the dried fennel in the olive oil. Pour in the soy sauce, place it in a dish and drizzle the honey over the top.

Remove the lamb from the pot and place in an ovenproof pan in the oven for 10 - 15 minutes to crisp the skin. After 5 minutes, add the fennel.

Strain the bay leaf, garlic, onion, shallot and thyme from the stock and reheat it. Remove the lamb and fennel from the oven. Place the fennel on the plates; reserving four pieces.

Slice the meat and place it on top of the fennel. Garnish with the reserved fennel and thyme. Pour a little of the reserved sauce over the top. Finish by placing a celeriac/celery root chip on each plate and serve.

Belly pork rolls in tomato sauce with herb oil

Prep and cook time: 40 minutes
Can be frozen
Serves: 4

Ingredients:
400 g | 1 lb belly pork, 8 thin slices
400 g | 1 lb veal schnitzel
8 small schnitzels, pounded thin
2 carrots, cut into 6 cm / 2 ½" sticks
1 stalk celery, cut into 6 cm / 2 ½" sticks
6 tbsp olive oil
1 shallot, finely chopped
100 ml | 7 tbsp dry white wine
250 g | 1 ¼ cups canned tomatoes, chopped
1 clove garlic, finely chopped
2 tbsp herbs (basil, parsley, rosemary), finely chopped

To garnish:
sprig rosemary

Method:

Lay the belly pork slices on the work surface and lay the schitzels on top. Place 1 carrot stick and one celery stick in the middle of each. Roll up and fix with a wooden tooth pick.

Heat 2 tbsp oil and fry the onion. Add the pork rolls and brown on all sides. Pour in the wine.

Add the tomatoes and season with salt and ground pepper. Cook gently for 15 minutes, stirring occasionally.

For the herb oil: mix the garlic with the herbs and the remaining oil.

Check the seasoning of the tomato sauce. Arrange the pork rolls on the sauce and drizzle herb oil over them. Garnish with rosemary and serve.

hot & spicy.

Thai green chicken curry

Prep and cook time: 1 hour 20 minutes
Can be frozen
Serves: 4

Ingredients:
For the green curry paste:
2 spring onions|scallions
2 green chilli peppers, deseeded and roughly chopped
2 cloves garlic, peeled
1 tsp fresh ginger, grated
1 tsp coriander seeds, crushed
1 stalk lemongrass, finely chopped
20 g | 1 cup Thai basil leaves
20 g | 1 cup coriander|cilantro leaves
3 tbsp olive oil
1 lime, juiced and grated zest

For the curry:
250 g | 1 ¼ cups Basmati rice
4 chicken breasts
2 tbsp peanut oil
400 ml | 1 ⅔ cups coconut milk
2 tbsp pistachios, chopped
2 kaffir lime leaves
1 red chilli pepper, thinly sliced
20 g | 1 cup coriander|cilantro leaves

Method:
Place all ingredients for the green curry paste in a blender and process to a smooth paste.

Cut the chicken breasts into bite size pieces, mix well with about 2 tbsp of the curry paste and marinate for 30 minutes.

Cook the rice according to the instructions on the packet.

Heat the peanut oil in a skillet and brown the meat on all sides for about 4 minutes.

Stir in the remaining curry paste, cook for 2 minutes and then pour in the coconut milk.

Add the pistachios, the kaffir lime leaves, chilli peppers and coriander/cilantro leaves. Bring to a boil, then simmer gently for 10 minutes. Season to taste with salt and serve with the rice.

Hot and sour chicken soup with omelette strips

Prep and cook time: 1 hour 30 minutes
Cannot be frozen
Serves: 4

Ingredients:
2 eggs
1 tbsp butter
1000 ml | 4 cups vegetable stock
2 tbsp sherry
2 tbsp soy sauce
2 tbsp white wine vinegar
1 tbsp sugar
1 bunch spring onions|scallions
2 carrots
4 chilli peppers
2 medium chicken breasts

To garnish:
coriander|cilantro leaves

Method:

Beat the egg with salt and pepper until foamy.

Melt the butter in a non-stick skillet and add the eggs so they cover the bottom of the skillet. Cook until they are becoming firm. Flip the omelette over and cook briefly. Place on a cutting board and roll up. With the seam face down, allow to cool.

Put the broth, sherry, soy sauce, vinegar and sugar in a saucepan and slowly bring to a boil.

Slice the spring onions/scallions half at an angle into thin rings and the other half into narrow strips.

Peel the carrots and slice them into narrow strips or slices.

Wash the chilli peppers and chop into thing rings.

Wash the chicken breasts, pat dry and cut into large pieces.

Put the chicken, spring onions/scallions, chillies and carrots into the soup and simmer for 30 minutes or until the meat is tender.

To serve, slice up the omelette and distribute it in the bowls. Season the soup with salt and pepper. Add soy sauce to taste if desired. Pour the soup over the omelette strips, garnish with the coriander/cilantro leaves and serve immediately.

Beef goulash with soured cream

Prep and cook time: 2 hours 20 minutes
Can be frozen
Serves: 4

Ingredients:
1 kg | 2 ¼ lbs braising beef, cubed
4 onions, chopped
3 tbsp vegetable oil
2 tbsp tomato paste
2 tbsp ground paprika
1 tsp ground caraway
250 ml | 1 cup dry red wine
400 ml | 1 ⅔ cups meat stock
2 red bell peppers, deseeded
and chopped
4 tbsp soured cream

Method:
Heat the oil in a large pan and seal the meat. Add the onions and fry until softened.

Add the tomato paste, paprika and caraway and pour in the red wine and stock.

Simmer over a low heat for around 1 ¼ hours, stirring occasionally.

Add the bell peppers to the goulash and simmer for a further 30 minutes until the meat is tender, adding a little more stock if it becomes too dry.

Season to taste with salt and pepper and serve with a swirl of soured cream.

Spicy lamb ribs

Prep and cook time: 1 hour 30 minutes Marinate: 4 hours
Cannot be frozen
Serves: 4

Ingredients:
2 kg | 2 ½ pounds breast of lamb,
with bones
2 garlic cloves
3 tbsp olive oil
6 tbsp tomato juice
1 tbsp tomato paste
4 tbsp honey
2 tbsp Tabasco
2 tbsp red wine vinegar
1 tbsp paprika powder, hot
1 tsp Cayenne pepper
1 tbsp pickled jalapeño peppers

Method:

Wash the breast of lamb and pat dry. Cut into portions containing two ribs each.

Peel the garlic and chop finely.

Heat the oil with the tomato juice, tomato paste and honey in a saucepan, stirring constantly, until the honey dissolves.

Mix together the Tabasco, red wine vinegar, paprika powder and Cayenne pepper.

Pat the jalapeños dry and mash them with a fork.
Combine them with the garlic and add them to the marinade. Season with salt and ground black pepper.

Add the lamb and marinate for at least 4 hours, or overnight if possible.

Preheat the oven to 180°C (160° fan) 350°F, gas 4.

Season the lamb breast pieces with salt and pepper and cook slowly for an hour, turning and basting frequently.

Spicy fish soup with sweet potato and chilli

Prep and cook time: 1 hour 10 minutes
Cannot be frozen
Serves: 4

Ingredients:
4 shallots, peeled and roughly chopped
2 carrots, peeled and chopped
400 g | 1 lb sweet potato, peeled and chopped
1 papaya, flesh chopped into cubes
2 stalks celery, sliced
2 red chilli peppers, deseeded and chopped into rings
2 tbsp oil
600 ml | 2 ½ cups fish stock
200 g | 1 cup tomatoes, chopped
4 tbsp cognac
2 tbsp sherry
2 1/2 cm Cayenne pepper
2 cloves
1 bay leaf
500 g | 1 ¼ lbs coley filet, dried and chopped into bite size pieces
1 sprig coriander|cilantro, chopped into strips

Method:

Heat the oil, add the shallots, chopped vegetables and papaya and soften.

Pour in the fish stock, tomatoes, cognac and sherry. Add the Cayenne pepper and cloves and just enough water to cover all ingredients and simmer the soup for 30 minutes.

Add the fish, coriander/cilantro and chilli, remove from the heat and leave to gently cook through for 6-8 minutes.

Season to taste with salt and pepper, ladle into bowls and serve with toasted bread.

Mooli moong dahl

Prep and cook time: 30 minutes Soak: 30 minutes
Cannot be frozen
Serves: 4

Ingredients:
150 g | 1 cup yellow mung beans,
rinsed and soaked for 30 minutes
250 g | 1 ¾ cups mooli|daikon,
peeled and finely grated
1 tsp turmeric
1 green chilli, chopped into fine rings
1 tbsp ghee
2 cloves
½ tsp cumin seeds
1 bay leaf
1 tsp fresh ginger, peeled and grated
Cayenne pepper

Method:
Boil the mung beans with the mooli/daikon and turmeric in 2 cups water for 20 minutes until the beans are soft.

Heat the ghee in a large skillet, add the chilli, cloves, cumin, bay leaf and ginger and fry briefly.

Add the cooked bean mixture, loosening with a little water if necessary, and simmer for 4-5 minutes.

Season with salt and Cayenne pepper to serve.

Chorizo with black beans and potatoes

Prep and cook time: 1 hour 30 minutes
Cannot be frozen
Serves: 4

Ingredients:

150 g | 1 cup dried black beans

200 g | 2 cups chorizo, sliced

400 g | 1 lb floury potatoes, peeled and quartered

1 green bell pepper, chopped

2 onions, chopped

2 cloves garlic, chopped

2 red chilli peppers, deseeded and sliced in half lengthwise

$\frac{1}{2}$ tsp dried thyme

2 tbsp olive oil

250 ml | 1 cup beef stock

100 g | $\frac{1}{2}$ cup canned tomatoes, chopped

2 tbsp fresh, chopped parsley

Method:

Soak the beans overnight in water. Wash and allow to drain.

Fry the chilli peppers, onion, garlic, chorizo and thyme in the hot oil until the onion is translucent.

Add the beef stock, tomatoes and beans and a little salt. Cover and simmer for approximately 30 minutes stirring occasionally.

Add the potatoes and chopped bell pepper. Simmer for 30 minutes more.

Stir in the parsley. Season with salt and pepper and serve.

Spicy peanut soup

Prep and cook time: 30 minutes
Can be frozen
Serves: 4

Ingredients:
1 shallot
1 garlic clove
1 chilli pepper
1 tbsp peanut oil
5 tbsp peanut butter
400 ml | 1 ²/₃ cups vegetable stock
100 ml | 7 tbsp coconut milk
soy sauce
Cayenne pepper

To garnish:
1 tbsp peanuts
1 chilli pepper

Method:

Peel and finely chop the shallot and garlic clove. Finely chop the chilli pepper. Place all three ingredients in a saucepan and sauté in hot oil.

Add the peanut butter. Continue cooking briefly and then add the stock and coconut milk. Cook for approximately 15 minutes, stirring occasionally, until creamy. Season to taste with the soy sauce and Cayenne pepper.

For the garnish, coarsely chop the peanuts and toast them in a dry saucepan. Put the soup in small bowls and sprinkle the tops with the peanuts and chilli pepper.

Andalucian fish soup

Prep and cook time: 40 minutes Marinating time: 2 hours
Cannot be frozen
Serves: 4

Ingredients:
500 g | 1 ¼ lbs monk fish fillets,
cut into chunks
1 shallot
2 cloves garlic
1 spring onion|scallion
1 chilli
1 sprig rosemary
4 tbsp olive oil
200 g | 2 cups chopped tomatoes
2 yellow bell peppers
1 tbsp basil leaves
4 sprigs thyme
400 ml | 1 ⅔ cups tomato juice
200 ml | ⅞ cup fish stock
Tabasco sauce

Method:
Peel the shallot and the garlic, finely chop the garlic and roughly chop the spring onion/scallion. Wash the chilli and cut into thin rings.

Remove some of the rosemary needles and finely chop.
Mix with 2 tbsp of the oil, chilli, garlic and fish and leave for 2 hours to marinate.

Wash the bell peppers, halve, de-seed and chop.
Finely chop the basil and thyme leaves. Save some of the leaves for the garnish.

Take the fish out of the marinade and fry in a skillet until golden brown, then remove.

Heat the remaining oil in a large pan and sauté the shallots. Add the bell pepper, the tomatoes and pour in the tomato juice and the fish stock. Simmer gently for 20 minutes.

Mix in the chopped herbs and season to taste with salt, pepper and Tabasco sauce. Place the fish in the soup and warm, then garnish with the remaining herbs and serve.

Spare ribs with devil sauce

Prep and cook time: 50 minutes
Cannot be frozen
Serves: 4

Ingredients:
2kg | 2 ½ lbs spare ribs
sunflower oil, for brushing
2 garlic cloves, chopped
1 onion, chopped
2 red chilli peppers, deseeded
and chopped
50 g | 2 tbsp honey
1 tsp salt
4 tbsp tomato paste
2 tbsp wine vinegar
2 tbsp Tabasco sauce

Method:

Cut the rib slab into individual ribs. Wash and pat dry.

Put the chilli peppers, onion, garlic, sugar, salt, a dash of pepper, tomato paste, vinegar and Tabasco in a saucepan and add 200 ml of water.

Bring to a boil. Simmer until smooth, about 10 minutes. Remove from heat and allow to cool.

Brush the ribs with a little oil and place them on a grill or under a hot broiler. Cook slowly for 20 minutes, turning occasionally.

Just before serving, brush the ribs with sauce.
Pass the remaining sauce at the table.

Red lentil soup with ginger, fennel and chilli

Prep and cook time: 30 minutes
Can be frozen
Serves: 4

Ingredients:
2 fennel bulbs, chopped
2 chilli peppers, deseeded and
chopped into fine rings
1 red onion, chopped
1 tsp fresh ginger, chopped
1 tbsp sesame oil
1 tsp curry powder
200 g | 1 cup red lentils
1000 ml | 4 cups vegetable stock

To garnish:
2 spring onions|scallions,
green parts only

Method:
Heat the oil in a skillet and cook the fennel, chilli and onion until softened. Add the curry powder and fry briefly.

Stir in the lentils and pour in the stock.

Cover and simmer over a low heat for 20 minutes until the lentils are soft.

Season with salt, ladle into bowls and serve garnished with the spring onion/scallion leaves.

Grilled shrimps in Creole sauce

Prep and cook time: 30 minutes
Cannot be frozen
Serves: 4

Ingredients:
1 onion, chopped
1 clove garlic, chopped
1 chilli pepper, deseeded and chopped
4 tbsp peanut oil
2 tbsp peanut butter
400 ml | 1 ⅔ cups chicken stock
1 tbsp ground paprika
2 tbsp crème fraiche
24 prawns|shrimps, peeled
apart from tail
lemon juice
1 tsp fresh thyme leaves

Method:

Heat 2 tbsp of the oil in a skillet and cook the onions until translucent. Add the chilli and garlic and fry for 3 minutes.

Stir in the peanut butter and allow to caramelize slightly.

Pour in the stock, add the paprika and simmer for 10 minutes until slightly thickened and reduced.

Stir in the crème fraiche and season to taste with salt, pepper and lemon juice.

Drizzle the prawns/shrimps with the remaining oil, season with salt and pepper and scatter with thyme.

Grill the shrimps on a hot griddle or barbeque for 3-4 minutes. Place in a bowl and pour over the sauce.

Serve with crusty white bread.

Korean kimchi soup

Prep and cook time: 1 hour 30 minutes Curing: 4-5 days
Cannot be frozen
Serves: 4

Ingredients:
1 large chinese cabbage
150 g | 1 cup rock salt
8 spring onions|scallions
2 garlic cloves
100 g | ¼ lb pickled mooli|daikon
2 red chilli peppers
1 tsp freshly grated ginger
1 tbsp sugar
800 ml | 3 ½ cups vegetable stock
light soy sauce

Method:
Slice the cabbage in half and chop into pieces of approximately 3 x 3 cm in size.

Using a large bowl, place a layer of cabbage in the bottom and sprinkle some salt on top. Continue adding layers of cabbage and salt. Finish with salt.

Cover the bowl with an inverted plate and weight it with a heavy object.

Place in a cool dark place for 4-5 days.

Pour off the fluid and wash the cabbage thoroughly under cold, running water. Carefully squeeze any additional water from the cabbage.

Remove the roots and any ragged ends from the spring onions /scallions and wash them. Cut into 3 cm / 1½" long pieces.

Peel the garlic cloves and finely chop them.

Thinly slice the mooli/daikon.

Wash the chilli peppers and slice them into rings.

Put the chilli peppers, spring onions/scallions, garlic, mooli/daikon, ginger and sugar into a pan and add the stock. Bring to a boil. Add the cabbage and continue cooking for approximately 20 minutes.

Season to taste with soy sauce and serve.

Curried tomatoes with eggs

Prep and cook time: 40 minutes
Cannot be frozen
Serves: 4

Ingredients:
2 onions, chopped
1 clove garlic, chopped
1 green chilli pepper, deseeded
and sliced into strips
3 tbsp ghee
½ tsp ground cumin
½ tsp ground turmeric
1 tsp ginger, peeled and grated
50 ml | 10 tsp cream
400 g | 2 cups tomatoes, chopped
1 tbsp tomato paste
1 tsp garam masala
½ tsp Cayenne pepper
8 hard-boiled eggs

To garnish:
coriander|cilantro leaves

Method:
Heat the ghee in a frying pan, stir in the cumin, turmeric and garam masala, then add the onion, garlic, ginger and chilli and fry gently until the onion and garlic are translucent.

Add the cream and stir in the chopped tomatoes, tomato paste and about 1 cup water. Simmer for 15 minutes. Add the Cayenne pepper and season to taste with salt.

Cut the eggs in half lengthwise, place in the curry sauce cut side up and garnish with coriander/cilantro leaves.

Mexican meatballs with spicy tomato sauce

Prep and cook time: 1 hour 10 minutes
Can be frozen
Serves: 4 (12 meatballs)

Ingredients:
For the meatballs:
1 slice of bread
3 tbsp cream
1 onion, finely chopped
1 tbsp olive oil
500 g | 1 ¼ lbs ground beef
1 egg
2 tbsp fresh, chopped parsley
a little lemon zest

For the tomato sauce:
2 shallots, finely chopped
1 garlic clove, finely chopped
400 g | 2 cups chopped tomatoes
2 red chilli peppers, deseeded and chopped
1 tbsp tomato paste
4 tbsp olive oil
200 ml | ⅞ cup red wine
sugar

Method:

Soften the bread in the cream and pull apart.

Sauté the chopped onion in the hot oil.

Put the ground beef, egg, parsley, softened bread, cooked onion and lemon zest in a bowl. Season with salt and pepper. Mix well by kneading. Form the mixture into small balls.

For the tomato sauce, sauté the chopped chillies, garlic and onions until transparent.

Stir in the tomato paste and deglaze with the red wine. Bring to a simmer.

Add the tomatoes and continue simmering for approximately 20 minutes. Stir occasionally.

Season with salt and pepper to taste.

Add the meat balls and cover the pan. Allow to steam gently for approximately 10 minutes.

Pork curry with fresh herbs

Prep and cook time: 1 hour 15 minutes
Can be frozen
Serves: 4

Ingredients:
700 g | 1 ¾ lbs lean pork
1 onion, chopped
1 dried chilli, chopped
3 tbsp oil
2 tsp finely grated fresh ginger
1/4 tsp ground coriander
1/2 tsp ground turmeric
1/4 tsp ground cumin
1/4 tsp ground cloves
2 tbsp dark soy sauce
1 tbsp chopped parsley
2 spring onions|scallions,
cut into rings

Method:
Wash the meat, pat dry and roughly dice.

Heat the oil in a large skillet and quickly brown the meat on all sides. Season with salt and pepper and add the onion, ginger and chilli.

Fry gently for about 3 minutes. Then stir in the coriander, turmeric, cumin and cloves, add 1 cup water and the soy sauce, cover and cook for 45 minutes. Add more water if necessary.

Serve sprinkled with parsley and spring onion/scallion rings.

Chicken Kerala

Prep and cook time: 1 hour 15 minutes
Can be frozen
Serves: 4

Ingredients:

4 cm | 1 ½" piece fresh ginger
(⅔ chopped, ⅓ sliced into fine strips)
1 tsp peppercorns, crushed
½ tsp ground turmeric
3 red onions, peeled (2 ½ chopped into
fine half-rings, ½ finely chopped)
2 chilli peppers
160 g | 3 cups coconut, grated
8 small potatoes, peeled and
chopped into bite-size pieces
3 tbsp oil
1 tbsp ghee
½ tsp mustard seeds
1 bay leaf
2 cloves garlic, sliced
1 cinnamon stick
4 cardamom pods
3 cloves
16 curry leaves
1 tsp curry powder
800 g | 2 lbs chicken, chopped
into bite-size pieces
125 ml | ½ cup vegetable stock
¼ tsp garam masala

Method:

Using a mortar and pestle, grind the chopped ginger, crushed pepper and turmeric to thick, coarse paste.

Puree the finely chopped onions with the chillies.

Place the coconut in a saucepan with 2 cups water, bring briefly to a boil and leave to steep for at least 15 minutes.

Line a sieve with muslin and pour in the coconut mixture. Squeeze well and reserve the coconut milk.

Boil the potatoes in plenty of water with a pinch of salt and turmeric for 25 minutes until soft.

Heat the oil (reserving 1 tbsp) with the ghee in a skillet and scatter in the mustard seeds. When the seeds begin to pop, add the bay leaf and fry lightly.

Add the onion, chilli, garlic, cinnamon stick and cardamom and fry briefly. After 20 seconds, add the ginger, cloves, curry leaves and curry powder.

Add the chicken to the spices, seal on all sides in a hot pan frying for 2-3 minutes and season with salt.

Add the potatoes, pour in the coconut milk and stock, stir in the strips of ginger and sprinkle with garam masala. Cover and cook for a further 20-30 minutes, stirring occasionally.

Fry the onion rings in the reserved oil until brown.

Serve the finished Kerala garnished with the fried onions.

desserts.

Bread pudding with rhubarb

Prep and cook time: 35 minutes
Can be frozen
Serves: 4

Ingredients:
1 medium stick rhubarb
50 ml | 10 tsp dry white wine
4 tbsp sugar
butter, for the baking dish
6 slices white bread
200 ml | 7/8 cup cream
4 eggs
seeds from a vanilla pod
1/2 tsp cinnamon
icing|confectioners' sugar, for dusting

Method:
Heat the oven to 200°C (180°C fan) 400°F, gas 6.

Wash and trim the rhubarb and cut into thin strips.
Bring the white wine to a boil, add the rhubarb and two tablespoons of sugar and simmer for 10 minutes.

Butter an ovenproof dish and arrange the bread neatly in the dish, overlapping the slices.

Whisk the cream with the eggs, vanilla seeds, cinnamon and the remaining sugar and pour over the bread.

Place the stewed rhubarb over the top and bake in the preheated oven for 20 minutes, until golden brown.
Dust with sugar before serving.

Riesling creams with apricot compote

Prep and cook time: 40 minutes Chilling time: 3 hours
Cannot be frozen
Serves: 4 (150 ml / ²/₃ cup moulds)

Ingredients:
1 lemon
200 ml | ⁷/₈ cup white wine (Riesling)
50 g | ¹/₄ cup sugar
½ tsp vanilla extract
200 ml | ⁷/₈ cup cream
5 leaves gelatine, soaked in cold water
150 g | 1 cup white chocolate, chopped

For the apricot compote:
100 g | ½ cup sugar
100 ml | 7 tbsp white wine (Riesling)
400 g | 2 ½ cups apricots, destoned and quartered
75 ml | ¹/₃ cup orange juice

To garnish:
50 g | ¹/₃ cup raspberries
Fresh mint leaves
4 spun sugar baskets

Method:
Grate a little zest from the lemon, squeeze and reserve the juice for the compote.

In a saucepan, simmer the white wine, sugar and vanilla extract for 5 minutes, add the cream, bring to a boil again and remove from the heat.

Squeeze the gelatine to remove excess liquid and dissolve in the hot cream. Add the chocolate and stir until dissolved.

Stand the mixing bowl in a larger bowl of cold water and stir the mixture until cooled. Spoon into moulds and chill for at least 3 hours.

To make the compote, heat the sugar in a saucepan, stirring until melted and caramelized. Deglaze with the Riesling, stirring to dissolve the caramel.

Add the apricots, orange juice and lemon juice, simmer for 8-10 minutes and let cool.

Turn the creams out of their moulds and arrange on plates with the compote.

To make spun sugar baskets, place 5 tbsp of sugar in a saucepan and caramelize until golden brown. Remove from the heat. Dip a fork into the caramel and draw threads of sugar across an oiled ladle bowl. Allow to set and gently remove from the ladle.

Garnish with raspberries, mint leaves and spun sugar baskets

Apple and blackberry pie

Prep and cook time: 1 hour 30 minutes
Cannot be frozen
Serves: 4

Ingredients:
For the pastry:
50 g | ¹/₂ cup plain|all purpose flour
4 tbsp spelt flour
50 g | ¹/₄ cup butter
2 tbsp sugar
1 egg yolk
1-2 tbsp cream

For the filling:
4 apples
200 g | 2 cups blackberries
150 ml | ²/₃ cup apple juice
200 ml | ⁷/₈ cup port
2 tbsp cornflour|cornstarch
75 g | ¹/₃ cup sugar
sugar, for sprinkling
200 ml | ⁷/₈ cup cream, whipped

Method:

Heat oven to 200°C (180°C fan) 400°F, gas 6.

Put all the pastry ingredients into a bowl and work to a smooth dough using the dough hook of an electric mixer. Wrap in foil or plastic wrap and chill.

Peel, quarter, core and dice the apples. Wash the blackberries and halve if necessary.

Put the juice into a pan with ¹/₂ cup port and bring to the boil. Mix the rest of the port smoothly with the cornflour/cornstarch and sugar, stir into the boiling liquid and return to the boil briefly.

Stir in the fruit, let cool slightly and put into the pie dish.

Roll out the pastry to a circle to fit the dish. Place on top of the filling, press the edges on firmly and bake in the preheated oven for 40 minutes.

Sprinkle with sugar and serve with whipped cream.

Chocolate terrine with raspberries

Prep and cook time: 30 minutes Freezing time: 4 hours
Can be frozen
Serves: 4

Ingredients:
150 g | 1 cup dark chocolate
(70% cocoa), chopped
2 egg yolks
2 tbsp sugar
2 sheets white gelatine
2 tbsp cocoa
20 ml | 4 tsp brandy
1 egg white
200 ml | ⅞ cup cream

To garnish:
50 ml | 10 tsp cream
a little cocoa powder
15 g | 1 tbsp dark chocolate, grated
200 g | 1 ½ cups raspberries
mint leaves

Method:
Melt the chocolate in a bowl placed over a pan of
simmering water.

Beat the egg yolks with 1 tbsp sugar until foamy and stir in the
cocoa and brandy.

Whisk the egg whites with the rest of the sugar until stiff.
Whip the cream until stiff. Gradually stir the melted chocolate
into the egg yolk mixture.

Fold in the cream, the beaten egg whites and the gelatine
(dissolved according to the package instructions).

Transfer to a longish mould that is lined with plastic wrap,
smooth the top and put into the refrigerator for at least 4 hours.

To serve, whip the cream with a little cocoa powder until
semi-stiff and pipe a small lattice on each dessert plate using
a decorators' bag with a plain nozzle. Sprinkle the terrine with
grated chocolate and serve on the plates with the raspberries.
Garnish with mint.

Rice pudding with plums and raisins

Prep and cook time: 1 hour
Cannot be frozen
Serves: 4

Ingredients:
600 g | 1 ½ lbs plums
800 ml | 3 ½ cups milk
4 tbsp sugar
250 g | 2 cups short grain rice
50 g | ⅓ cup raisins
cinnamon sugar, for sprinkling

Method:

Preheat the oven to 200°C (180°C fan) 400°F, gas 6.

Wash and de-stone the plums, then cut in half.

Bring the milk with the sugar and salt to a boil. Add the rice. Bring to a boil again while stirring.

Pour the rice into a stoneware dish. Sprinkle the raisins over the top and then add the plums. Bake in the preheated oven for 20-30 minutes.

Dust with the cinnamon sugar and serve.

Apricot dumplings

Prep and cook time: 1 hour 10 minutes
Cannot be frozen
Makes: 12-15 dumplings

Ingredients:
800 g | 2 lbs floury potatoes, peeled
250 g | 2 cups plain|all purpose flour
2 eggs
1 kg | 2 ½ lbs apricots
1 sugar cube per apricot
100 g | ½ cup butter
100 g | 1 cup breadcrumbs
2 tbsp icing|confectioners' sugar

Method:
Halve or quarter potatoes, depending on their size.
Boil in salted water for 30 minutes until soft. Drain, press through a ricer and let cool.

Mix the potatoes with the flour, eggs and salt and knead to a smooth dough.

Half and de-stone the apricots then push a sugar cube into the centre cavity of each one.

On a floured work surface roll the dough to a sausage around 6 cm / 1" thick and cut into 3 cm / 1" slices.

Flatten each slice of dough slightly and press an apricot into the middle. Mould the dough around the apricot and press closed to form a dumpling.

Place the dumplings in boiling salted water, remove from the heat and leave to poach gently for around 10 minutes.

Heat the butter in a skillet, add the breadcrumbs and fry until golden brown. Remove from the heat, add the sugar and roll each dumpling in the breadcrumb mixture.

Serve garnished with mint leaves and dusted with icing/confectioners' sugar.

Strawberry pancake cake

Prep and cook time: 25 minutes Cooking time: 40 minutes
Cannot be frozen
Serves: 4

Ingredients:
For the strawberry and vanilla cream:
500 ml | 2 cups milk
1 vanilla pod
5 egg yolks
100 g | ½ cup sugar
4 tbsp flour

For the pancakes:
300 g | 2 cups strawberries
2 eggs
2 egg yolks
250 ml | 1 cup milk
100 g | 1 cup flour
1 tbsp sugar
80 ml | ⅓ cup cream
¼ tsp salt
butter, for frying

Method:
For the strawberry and vanilla cream, put the milk into a pan, slit the vanilla pod open lengthwise, scrape out the seeds and stir into the milk with the pod.

Bring to the boil. Put the egg yolks and sugar into a bowl and beat until creamy, gradually mixing in the flour.

Stir the boiling milk into the egg yolk mixture, return to the pan, remove the vanilla pod and heat, beating constantly until creamy (do not allow to boil).

Strain the vanilla cream through a sieve and leave to cool, sprinkling the surface thinly with sugar to prevent a skin from forming.

Wash and hull the strawberries and finely puree about ⅓ of them. Push through a sieve. Mix the strawberry puree with half of the vanilla cream. Cut the remaining strawberries into smaller pieces.

For the pancakes, whisk the eggs, egg yolks and milk. Sieve the flour over and stir to produce a smooth batter. Stir in the cream and salt and leave to stand for 20 minutes.

Heat a little butter in a skillet, add 3-4 tbsp batter and cook for about 2 minutes each side over a medium heat. Repeat with the rest of the batter. Keep the pancakes warm.

When they are all ready spread the pancakes alternately with strawberry and vanilla cream and pile on top of each other. Serve with the strawberries and the remaining cream.

Syllabub with apples, nuts and caramel

Prep and cook time: 30 minutes
Cannot be frozen
Serves: 4

Ingredients:
2 apples, peeled, cored and chopped
$\frac{1}{2}$ tsp cinnamon
4 tbsp brown sugar
300 ml | 1 $\frac{1}{3}$ cups strong cider

For the cream:
2 tbsp sugar
4 tbsp strong cider
200 ml | $\frac{7}{8}$ cup cream

For the caramel:
50 g | $\frac{1}{4}$ cup sugar
2 tbsp chopped hazelnuts (cob nuts)
oil, for the plate

Method:

Mix the cinnamon and brown sugar and mix with the apple pieces and cider.

For the cream, dissolve the sugar in the cider. Beat the cream until stiff with an electric hand mixer then fold in the cider.

For the caramel, put the sugar into a pan with 4 tbsp water and boil to produce a light brown caramel. Stir in the nuts and pour on to an oiled plate. Leave to set.

To serve, half fill four glasses with apple mix and cover with whipped cream. Break the caramel into pieces and use to garnish the desserts.

Pineapple, passion fruit and papaya compote

Prep and cook time: 35 minutes
Cannot be frozen
Serves: 4

Ingredients:
400 ml | 1 ⅔ cups orange juice
1 clove
1 bay leaf
2 tbsp icing|confectioners' sugar
2 g | ½ tsp arrowroot
400 g | 1 lb ripe papaya
400 g | 1 lb pineapple flesh
2 ripe passion fruits

Method:

Heat the orange juice with the clove, bay leaf and sugar.

Stir in the arrowroot. Simmer and stir for about a minute.

Remove the clove and bay leaf.

Peel the papaya. Slice in half and remove the seeds.

Roughly chop the papaya and pineapple into pieces.
Put in a bowl.

Cut the passion fruit in half. Add the seeds, pulp and juice to the papaya and pineapple.

Pour the thickened juice over the top, mix carefully and put into individual bowls.

Serve warm or cold.

Sticky toffee and walnut pudding

Prep and cook time: 2 hour 30 minutes
Can be frozen
Serves: 4

Ingredients:
For the puddings:
125 ml | ½ **cup cream**
½ **vanilla pod**
50 g | ¼ **cup butter**
80 g | ⅔ **cup millet flour, freshly ground**
4 **egg whites**
3 **egg yolks**
50 g | ⅓ **cup ground walnuts**
50 g | ¼ **cup sugar**
butter, for the basins
50 g | ⅓ **cup ground almonds**

For the sauce:
3 **tbsp butter**
100 g | ½ **cup sugar**
50 g | ½ **cup pecans**
50 g | ½ **cup walnuts**
4 **tbsp cognac**

Method:

Heat the oven to 200°C (180°C fan) 375°F, gas 5.

Heat the cream in a pan. Slit the vanilla pod open lengthwise and scrape the seeds into the cream.

Heat the butter in another pan and stir in the millet flour. Add the vanilla-flavoured cream and heat, stirring, until the mixture forms a ball.

Remove from the heat, leave to cool slightly and stir in 1 egg white. Gradually stir in the egg yolks and the walnuts, then let cool.

Beat the remaining egg whites until they form soft peaks, trickling in the sugar, and continue beating until firm and glossy. Then carefully fold the beaten egg white into the millet mixture.

Grease 4 small ovenproof bowls and sprinkle with ground almonds. Divide the mixture between the bowls. Seal the bowls with foil, then stand them in a roasting tin or baking pan and fill with water to a depth of 3 cm below the rim of the bowls. Put into the oven and cook the puddings for 1 ¾ hours.

For the sauce, melt the butter and sugar in a pan over a medium heat. Stir over the heat until the sugar begins to caramelize. Roughly chop the pecans and walnuts and add to the pan as soon as the sugar begins to brown.

Caramelize the nuts briefly, then slowly stir in ½ cup water and cook until the sauce has a syrupy consistency. Remove the caramel and nut sauce from the heat and add cognac to taste.

Take the puddings out of the bain marie, remove the foil and leave the puddings to stand for about 5 minutes. To serve, run the point of a knife around the top of the bowls and turn the puddings out on to 4 plates. Take the nuts out of the toffee sauce, place on top of the puddings and drizzle the rest of the sauce over. Serve warm.

Poached pears, rhubarb and peaches in syrup

Prep and cook time: 30 minutes
Cannot be frozen
Serves: 4

Ingredients:
4 small pears
4 small peaches
2 stalks medium rhubarb
100 g | ½ cup sugar
100 ml | 7 tbsp port
1 orange, juice and peel
200 ml | ⅞ cup dry red wine
2 cloves
1 cinnamon stick

To garnish:
2 tbsp honey
2 tbsp nut brittle

Method:
Peel, halve and core the pears. Wash, quarter and stone the peaches. Wash and trim the rhubarb and cut at an angle into approximately 4 cm/1 ½ lengths.

Put the sugar into a pan and heat until it caramelises. Stir in the port, orange juice and red wine.

Add the cloves, cinnamon stick, orange peel and pears. Poach for about 5 minutes then add the peaches and rhubarb.

Cover and poach for a further 5 minutes. Then take the fruit out of the liquid and simmer gently, stirring occasionally, until the liquid has the consistency of syrup. Remove the cinnamon, cloves and orange peel and let cool slightly.

Arrange the fruit on plates and add a little of the still-warm syrup. Drizzle with a little honey, sprinkle with nut brittle and serve.

Baked apples and custard

Prep and cook time: 1 hour 15 minutes
Cannot be frozen
Serves: 4

Ingredients:
For the custard:
500 ml | 2 cups milk
¹/₂ tsp vanilla extract
2 - 3 tsp corn cornflour|cornstarch
4 tbsp sugar
1 egg yolk

For the baked apples:
75 g | ¹/₂ cup flaked|slivered almonds
2 tsp raisins
3 tbsp icing|confectioners' sugar
1/2 tsp ground cinnamon
50 g | ¹/₂ cup marzipan paste,
finely chopped
4 cooking apples, cored
butter, to grease the dish
2 tbsp butter
icing|confectioners' sugar to dust

Method:

Heat the oven to 200°C (180°C fan) 400°F, gas 6.

To make the custard, reserve 3-4 tbsp of milk, bring the remaining milk to a boil with the vanilla extract and remove from the heat.

Combine the sugar and corn cornflour/cornstarch and mix to a smooth paste with the reserved milk. Stir in the egg yolk and combine well.

Stir the egg mixture into the cooled milk and return to the heat. Heat the mixture, stirring constantly until it thickens and becomes a smooth sauce. Let it cool, stirring occasionally.

To make the filling, mix half the almonds with the raisins, 1 tbsp of icing/confectioners' sugar, the cinnamon and the chopped marzipan.

Fill the apples with the mixture and place in a buttered, ovenproof dish. Dust with the remaining sugar, dot with butter and bake for 30-40 minutes.

Remove from the oven and arrange on plates. Pour over the custard, scatter with the remaining flaked/slivered almonds and serve dusted with icing/confectioners' sugar.

Spiced steamed pudding

Prep and cook time: 3 hours 30 minutes
Can be frozen
Serves: 4

Ingredients:
150 g | 1 cup golden raisins
150 g | 1 cup currants
100 g | ½ cup prunes
400ml | 1 ½ cups rum
1 apple, peeled, cored and quartered
50 g | ¼ cup candied lemon peel
50 g | ¼ cup candied orange peel
4 tbsp butter, softened
75 g | ¾ cup bread crumbs
75 g | ¾ cup plain|all purpose flour
75 g | ½ cup ground hazelnuts
(cob nuts)
50 g | ¼ cup brown sugar
3 eggs
¼ tsp ground cloves
½ tsp cinnamon
molasses, for pouring over the top

Method:
Preheat the oven to 160°C (140°C fan) 325°F, gas 2.

Blanch the raisins and currants. Place in a sieve and drain well.

Finely chop the prunes and mix with the sultanas, currants and rum.

Finely grate the apple.

Mix together the apple, rum-fruit mixture, candied lemon and orange peel.

Add the softened butter, bread crumbs, flour, nuts, eggs, clove and sugar to the fruit mixture and mix together to form a batter.

Fill a buttered, ovenproof bowl with the batter and cover the top with a lid or foil. Put the pudding on a rack (this ensures even cooking) in a hot water bath and steam in the oven for approximately 3 hours. Add more water if necessary.

When ready to serve, remove the pudding from the bowl. Drizzle a little molasses over the top if desired.

Pancakes with elderberry and plum compote

Prep and cook time: 45 minutes
Cannot be frozen
Serves: 4

Ingredients:
For the compote:
400 ml | 1 ²/₃ cups elderberry juice
50 g | ¼ cup sugar
1 cinnamon stick
2 cloves
1 lemon, juiced
250m l 1 cup plum brandy
1 kg | 2 ¼ lbs plums

For the pancakes:
75 ml | ⅓ cup buttermilk
1 egg
1 tbsp sugar
40 g | ⅓ cup plain|all purpose flour
½ tsp baking powder
2 tbsp butter

To garnish:
elderberries
icing|confectioners' sugar

Method:

For the compote, put the elderberry juice, sugar, cinnamon, lemon juice and plum brandy in a saucepan. Bring to a boil. Reduce heat and continue simmering until the mixture thickens, for 15 minutes.

Wash the plums, halve them and remove the stones. Add them to the saucepan, cook for 5 minutes then remove from heat and allow to cool. Take out the cinnamon stick.

For the pancakes combine the buttermilk with the egg and sugar. Mix well.

Sift the flour with the baking powder. Add to the milk mixture and mix until it forms a thick batter.

For the pancakes, heat the butter in a skillet and pour in tablespoons of batter, a few at a time. Fry the pancakes for about one minute until golden brown. Turn and fry for another minute until done. Drain on paper towels.

Divide the compote amongst the plates and place the pancakes on top. Garnish with the elderberries and dust with sugar.

Poppy seed dumplings with fruit compote

Prep and cook time: 1 hour 45 minutes
Can be frozen
Serves: 4

Ingredients:
For the compote:
1 cinnamon stick
1 lemon, peeled
1 star anise
250 ml | 1 cup elderberry juice
50 ml | 10 tsp dry red wine
sugar, as needed
100 g | ½ lb plums
100 g | ½ lb blackberries
100 g | ½ lb elderberries
2 pears

For the dumplings:
275 g | 2 ½ cups plain|all purpose flour
50 g | 1 tbsp poppy seeds
1 tsp dried yeast
150 ml | ⅔ cup milk
3-4 tsp sugar
½ tsp salt
1 egg
50 g | ¼ cup melted butter

Method:

For the compote, add the cinnamon, lemon peel and star anise to the elderberry juice and bring to a boil.

Add the wine and sweeten with sugar to taste.
Cover and let steep for at least 20 minutes.

Wash the plums, blackberries and elderberries and let them dry. Halve the plums and remove the stones.

Peel the pears, halve them, remove the cores and slice diagonally into bite-size pieces.

Reheat the juice/wine mix almost to boiling. Carefully add the pears and plums and let them cook 3-4 minutes until they are nearly cooked.

Add the elderberries and cook for another minute. Finally, mix in the blackberries and remove the compote from the stove. Pour into a bowl and remove the cinnamon, star anise and lemon peel. Let cool.

For the dumplings, mix the flour, poppy seeds and yeast together. Heat the milk until lukewarm and add to the flour.

Add the sugar, salt and egg to the flour as well and knead the mixture into a semi-firm dough. Place the dough on a floured tray or table and work it into a long roll.

Cut the roll of dough into 16 equal pieces. Shape each piece of dough into a round dumpling.

Use half the butter to coat a baking pan and place the dumplings in the pan, leaving space for each to expand. Place in a warm place and allow the dough to prove for 30 minutes.

Heat the oven to 180°C (160°C fan) 375°F, gas 5.

Coat the dumplings with the remaining butter and bake in the preheated oven for 30-40 minutes, until golden-brown. Serve with the compote.

Polenta pudding with currants

Prep and cook time: 25 minutes Chilling time: 2 hours
Cannot be frozen
Serves: 4

Ingredients:
500 ml | 2 cups milk
¼ tsp salt
80 g | ⅕ cup polenta
3 eggs
80 g | ⅓ cup sugar
300 g | 3 cups redcurrants
150 g | 3 cups blackcurrants
3 tbsp sugar

Method:
Put the milk into a pan with the salt and bring to the boil. Sprinkle in the polenta and stir over a low heat until the thickened mixture will drop from a spoon.

Separate the eggs. Stir the egg yolks into the polenta with 2 tbsp sugar.

Whisk the egg whites stiffly with the rest of the sugar and carefully fold into the polenta. Transfer to 4 small buttered moulds and chill for 2 hours.

Strip the currents from their stalks and put into a pan. Add the sugar and a little water and simmer over a low heat for 5 minutes.

Turn the puddings out of their moulds and serve with the blackcurrants and redcurrants.

Rhubarb rice cake

Prep and cook time: 1 hour
Cannot be frozen
Serves: 4

Ingredients:
350 g | 3 ½ cups rhubarb, diced
100 g | ½ cup sugar
50 g | ⅓ cup golden raisins
400 ml | 1 ⅔ cups milk
100 ml | 7 tbsp cream
zest of 1 lemon, finely grated
200 g | 1 ⅓ cup short grain rice
2 eggs

Method:
Heat the oven to 200°C (180°C fan) 400°F, gas 6.

Sprinkle the rhubarb with 2 tbsp sugar, leave for 10 minutes to steep.

Mix the golden raisins with the rhubarb pieces.

Bring the milk, cream, lemon zest and remaining sugar to a boil and add the rice.

Reduce the heat to the lowest setting and continue to cook, stirring constantly, until the rice is al denté (about 15 minutes). If the liquid reduces too much, add a little water.

Remove from the heat and stir in the eggs.

Grease a loaf pan with butter and spoon in one third of the rice. Spoon in the rhubarb mixture and cover with the rest of the rice.

Bake for 25 minutes and let cool slightly.

Turn out of the loaf pan, cut into slices and serve warm.

Apricot and berry pudding with almonds

Prep and cook time: 40 minutes
Cannot be frozen
Serves: 4

Ingredients:
8 apricots
200 g | 1 ¼ cups raspberries
4 stalks redcurrants
2 eggs
500 g | 2 cups quark
(low-fat soft cheese)
30 g | ¼ cup cornflour|cornstarch
3 tbsp sugar
1 tbsp flaked|slivered almonds

Method:

Heat the oven to 200°C (180°C fan) 400°F, gas 6.

Wash the fruit. Halve the apricots, remove the stones and cut each half into quarters. Carefully wash and dry the raspberries. Wash the redcurrants.

Separate the eggs and beat the egg whites until stiff.

Mix the quark smoothly with the cornflour/cornstarch, sugar and egg yolks. Then fold in the beaten egg whites.

Divide the quark mixture between 4 small ovenproof dishes, scatter the fruit over, press in lightly and bake in the preheated oven for 15-20 minutes.

Serve hot sprinkled with flaked/slivered almonds.

Chocolate ravioli with strawberry sauce

Prep and cook time: 1 hour 20 minutes
Cannot be frozen
Serves: 4

Ingredients:
For the dough:
200 g | 2 cups plain|all purpose flour
100 g | ¾ cups ground almonds
160 g | ⅔ cups butter
80 g | ⅔ cup icing|confectioners' sugar
½ lemon, grated rind
4 egg yolks

For the filling:
40 g | ⅓ cup dark chocolate
(70% cocoa), chopped
150 g | ⅔ cup ricotta
40 g | ½ cup crumbled
amaretti biscuits
2 tbsp sugar

For the strawberry sauce:
300 g | 2 cups strawberries
50 g | ¼ cup sugar

Method:
Heat the oven to 180°C (160°C fan) 475°F, gas 5.

For the dough, chop the ingredients together and mix to a smooth dough. Cover and chill for 30 minutes.

For the filling, melt the broken chocolate in a bowl placed over a pan of simmering water, then mix with the ricotta, amaretti crumbs and sugar and chill for 30 minutes.

For the sauce, wash and hull the strawberries and cook with the sugar and ½ cup of water for about 5 minutes. Push through a sieve and allow it to cool.

Roll the dough out thinly on a floured work surface and cut in half. Cover one half with teaspoonfuls of the filling, evenly spaced 5 cm / 2" apart.

Lay the second half on top. Press together between the piles of filling and cut out 6 squares using a pastry wheel.

Place on a cookie sheet lined with baking parchment and bake in the preheated oven for 20 minutes.

Take out and cool on a cake rack. Serve the ravioli on plates with strawberry sauce.

Steamed jam sponge pudding

Prep and cook time: 1 hour 30 minutes
Cannot be frozen
Serves: 4

Ingredients:
4 tbsp cherry jam
125 g | ²/₃ cup butter
125 g | ¹/₂ cup sugar
2 eggs
¹/₂ tbsp vanilla extract
175 g | 1 ³/₄ cups self-raising flour
1 tsp baking powder
50 ml | 10 tsp milk
butter for greasing

To garnish:
mint leaves

Method:
Lightly grease 4, 250ml / ¹/₂ pint ovenproof bowls with butter. Put 1 tbsp of jam in the bottom of each.

Sift the baking powder with the flour.

Beat the butter with sugar until fluffy. Gradually adding the eggs until well incorporated.

Add the vanilla extract, sifted dry ingredients and milk; mix to form a smooth batter.

Fill the moulds with the batter and smooth the tops.

Lightly grease small pieces of tin foil with some butter. With the buttered side face down, cover the bowls and wrap well.

Sit the bowls on the bottom of a large pot or roasting pan. Fill with boiling water halfway up the sides of the bowls, cover and allow to steam for approximately 1 hour, adding more boiling water as necessary.

To serve, remove the puddings from the bowls and garnish with mint.

Crispy fried caramelized apple wedges

Prep and cook time: 30 minutes
Cannot be frozen
Serves: 4

Ingredients:
4 apples
100 g | ¾ cup cornflour|cornstarch
vegetable oil, for frying
60 g | ⅓ cup sugar

Method:

Peel, core and cut the apples into small wedges.

Put the cornflour/cornstarch in a flat dish. Dredge the apple wedges in the cornflour/cornstarch.

Heat the oil in a saucepan. To test if the oil is hot enough, put the handle of a cooking spoon into the hot oil. If bubbles begin to form, it's ready. Add the apple wedges and fry until gold brown – approximately 3 minutes.

Transfer the fried apple to paper towels.

Over a low flame, put the sugar in a clean pan and very carefully add 2 to 3 tablespoons of water. Stir continuously until the sugar melts and the caramel begins to bubble. Put the apples back in the pan and coat them with the caramel.

Immediately divide the apples evenly among the dishes. Garnish with mint.

Catalan cream with raspberries

Prep and cook time: 40 minutes Chilling time: 4 hours
Cannot be frozen
Serves: 4

Ingredients:
500 ml | 2 cups milk
150 g | ¾ cup sugar
1 lemon, grated peel
1 cinnamon stick
4 egg yolks
20 g | 2 tbsp cornflour|cornstarch
25 ml | 5 tsp pastis
200 g 1 ¼ cups fresh raspberries

Method:

Mix 1 tbsp of the milk with the egg yolks and cornflour/cornstarch.

Put the remaining milk, ½ cup of the sugar, the lemon peel and cinnamon stick in a pan and bring to a boil.

Lower the heat, remove the cinnamon stick and gradually beat in the egg yolk mix. Stir until thickened but do not allow to boil. Add the pastis.

Place the mixture in shallow bowls. Sprinkle with the raspberries and allow to cool. For best results, prepare before midday and allow to rest in a cool room.

Shortly before serving, sprinkle the rest of the sugar over the desserts. Caramelize using a kitchen blow torch or brown under a hot grill.

Profiteroles with chocolate sauce

Prep and cook time: 1 hour
Can be frozen
Makes: 30 - 35 profiteroles

Ingredients:
For the profiteroles:
¹/₂ tsp salt
50 g | ¹/₂ cup butter
150 g | 1 ¹/₄ cup plain|all purpose flour
1 - 2 tbsp cornflour|cornstarch
1 tsp baking powder
4 eggs

For the chocolate sauce:
300 g | 2 cups dark
chocolate, chopped
200 ml | ⁷/₈ cup cream

Method:

Heat the oven to 200°C (180°C fan) 375°F, gas 5.

For the profiteroles, put 1 cup water in a large pan.
Have the rest of the ingredients ready.

Put the salt and butter into the water and bring to a boil.
Mix the flour, cornflour/cornstarch and baking powder together
and add them all at once to the boiling water.

Stir constantly over a medium heat until a large round ball of
dough forms and a white film forms on the bottom of the pan.

Put the dough in a bowl and allow to cool for 5 minutes.
Using the dough hook of an electric hand mixer, add the eggs
one at a time until well incorporated.

Line a cookie sheet with baking parchment. Put the dough in
a decorators' bag with a large nozzle and squeeze 30-35 balls
onto the baking sheet.

Bake for 15-20 minutes. Remove and allow it to cool.

For the sauce, coarsely chop the chocolate.
Place in a bowl over gently simmering water and add the
cream. Melt the chocolate while stirring. Let cool slightly.
Serve warm with the profiteroles.

preserves.

Spiced greengages

Prep and cook time: 30 minutes
Cannot be frozen
Serves: 4

Ingredients:
1 orange
1 sprigs rosemary
2 tsp olive oil
500 g | 1 ¼ lbs greengages
3 tbsp sugar
1 tsp crushed black pepper corns

Method:

Wash the orange in hot water and pat dry. Finely grate the peel and squeeze out the juice.

Remove the rosemary leaves from the stem and chop finely.

Wash the greengages. Slice in half and remove the stones. Press the cut sides firmly into the sugar.

Heat a pan and pour in the oil.

Put the greengages, sugar side down, in the hot pan and allow to caramelize.

Deglaze the pan with the orange juice so the caramelized pieces come unstuck.

Add the orange peel, rosemary and crushed pepper and stir.

The perfect accompaniment to serve with Brie and cantuccini cookies.

Gooseberry and cherry marmalade

Prep and cook time: 45 minutes Steeping time: 3 hours
Cannot be frozen
Makes: 5 small jars

Ingredients:
500 g | 3 cups gooseberries,
topped and tailed
500 g | 2 cups cherries, pitted
1 kg | 5 cups sugar
1 lemon, juiced and zest grated

Method:
Mash one half of the gooseberries and one half of the cherries with a fork to a coarse puree.

Then mix all of the fruit with the preserving sugar and allow to steep for at least 3 hours.

Bring the fruit mixture to a boil slowly, stirring frequently. Bring to a rolling boil and cook for 20-30 minutes until the temperature reaches 105°C / 220°F.

To sterilize the jars, fill with boiling water and let stand for 5 minutes. Discard the water and fill the jars with marmalade.

Pickled cucumbers

Prep and cook time: 30 minutes Marinading time: 24 hours
Cannot be frozen
Makes: 4 large jars

Ingredients:
2000 g | 4 ½ lbs pickling cucumbers
2 tbsp salt
1 tsp white peppercorns
1 tsp allspice seeds
1 tbsp mustard seeds
2 dried red chillies
a little freshly chopped dill
3 shallots
750 ml | 3 cups white wine vinegar
100 g | ½ cup sugar

Method:
Pierce the cucumbers all over with a needle. Place in a bowl, sprinkle with the salt and cover with water.
Allow to sit for 24 hours.

Drain the water. Rinse the cucumbers and pat dry.

Divide the cucumbers equally between the jars.

Mix together the peppercorns, allspice seeds, mustard seeds, chilli peppers and dill. Divide equally between the jars.

Peel the shallots and cut into small wedges. Divide equally among the jars.

Bring the vinegar, sugar and 3 cups water to a boil. Pour over the cucumbers. Close the jars tightly and store in a cool place.

Wait 4-6 weeks before using.

Red fig preserve

Prep and cook time: 25 minutes Steeping time: 2 hours
Cannot be frozen
Makes: 4 small jars

Ingredients:
1 kg | 2 lbs ripe figs
1 kg | 2 lbs preserving sugar
100 ml | 7 tbsp ruby port
juice and zest of 1 lemon

Method:
Wash, clean and dice the figs. Mix with the preserving sugar and allow to steep for 2 hours.

Place fruit in a saucepan, add the port and bring to a boil while stirring. Bring to a rolling boil and allow to cook for. 1 hour, stirring frequently. Test by dropping a smear onto a chilled plate; if the mixture crinkles when you push it with your finger, it is ready.

To sterilize the jars, fill with boiling water, let stand for 5 minutes and discard water.

Fill jars with the preserve and close. Turn the jars upside down for about 15 minutes then turn them right side up and allow to cool.

Apricot, kiwi and mint jam

Prep and cook time: 1 hour 30 minutes
Cannot be frozen
Makes: 6 medium jars

Ingredients:
2 sprigs mint
700 g | 1 ¾ lbs fresh apricots
3 kiwis
juice of 1 lemon
500 g | 1 ¼ cups sugar

Method:

Cut the mint leaves into narrow strips.

Halve the apricots. Remove the pits and chop.

Slice the kiwis into eighths.

Mix the apricots, lemon juice and sugar in a large bowl. Cover and allow to rest for 30 minutes so a juice forms.

Put the apricot mix in a large pot. Bring to a boil and continue to cook for 30 minutes, stirring frequently.

Stir in the kiwis and mint.

Fill the jars to the top with the jam and close immediately.

Turn the jars upside down for 5 minutes. Then turn the right side up and allow to cool.

Pickled beets

Prep and cook time: 1 hour 30 minutes
Cannot be frozen
Makes: 4 medium pint jars

Ingredients:
600 g | ½ lb red beets
200 g | ½ lb white cabbage
salt
5 cm | 2" fresh ginger
5 cm | 2" piece horseradish root
1 chilli pepper, deseeded
and finely sliced
400 ml | 1 ⅔ cups apple vinegar
60 g | ¼ cup sugar
1 cinnamon stick
2 cooking apples

Method:
Boil the beets for approximately 40 minutes until you can pierce them easily with a knife. Peel and let cool.
Slice into narrow strips.

Decore the cabbage and remove any old leaves. Slice into narrow strips and blanch in boiling salted water for 2-3 minutes. Immerse in cold water and drain.

Peel and finely chop the ginger and horseradish.

Put the vinegar, sugar, cinnamon, horseradish, ginger, chilli and 2 cups water in a saucepan. Bring to a boil and continue cooking for 5 minutes.

Peel, halve, de-core and finely grate the apples.

Put the beets, apple and cabbage into the hot liquid. Bring to the boil again.

Fill the clean jars and close tightly.

Wait three days before using.

Quince compote with vanilla

Prep and cook time: 45 minutes
Cannot be frozen
Makes: 2 jars

Ingredients:
14 quinces
juice of half a lemon
2 vanilla pods
150 g | ¾ cup brown sugar
1 clove
250 ml | 1 cup water
150 ml | ⅔ cup dry white wine

Method:

Peel, deseed and cut the quinces into wedges.

Put the fruit into a bowl and drizzle the lemon juice over the top.

Cut the vanilla pods open lengthwise and scrape out the seeds.

Put the seeds, sugar, clove, water and wine into a pot and bring to a boil.

Add the quince wedges and cover. Simmer for approximately 30 minutes until tender but not mushy (cooking time may vary).

Serve warm as a dessert or preserve in jars.

Lemon marmalade

Prep and cook time: 35 minutes
Cannot be frozen
Makes: 7 - 8 small jars

Ingredients:
2500 g | 5 ½ lbs lemons
1 kg | 2 lbs sugar

Method:

Wash the lemons with hot water and rub dry.

Remove long wide strips of peel from three or four of the lemons with a peeler. Slice these long, wide strips into very thin strips.

Squeeze all the lemons.

Put the juice and lemon peel into a large pot, add the preserving sugar and stir well.

Bring to a boil over high heat, stirring constantly.

Bring to a rolling boil and continue cooking and stirring for 4 minutes longer.

Decant into jars and close tightly.

Pickled onions

Prep and cook time: 20 minutes
Cannot be frozen
Makes: 2 large jars

Ingredients:
1 kg | 2 lbs small white onions
500 ml | 2 cups dry white wine
500 ml | 2 cups apple vinegar
3 tsp salt
3 tsp sugar
5 black peppercorns
1 tsp mustard seeds
2 chilli peppers
2 bay leaves
a little fresh dill

Method:

Peel the onions and divide them equally between the two jars.

Put the wine, vinegar, salt, sugar, peppercorns, mustard seeds, chilli peppers, bay leaf and dill into a saucepan and bring to a boil.

Simmer for 5 minutes then pour over the onions so that they are completely covered.

Tightly close the jars.

Preserve for at least two weeks before using; they will last for at least 6 months.

Pumpkin preserve

Prep and cook time: 1 hour
Cannot be frozen
Makes: 4 jars

Ingredients:
1½ kg | 3 ¼ lbs pumpkin
1 lemon
1 orange
100 ml | 7 tbsp apple juice
1 tbsp freshly grated ginger
500 g | 2 ½ cups preserving sugar

Method:
Peel the pumpkin and remove the seeds. Cut the pumpkin flesh (there should be about 1 kg / 2 lbs) into narrow wedges.

Squeeze the juice from the lemon and the orange.

Put the pumpkin, ginger, lemon, orange and apple juices into a saucepan and bring to a boil. Stir occasionally. Cook for approximately 20 minutes until soft but not mushy.

Stir in the preserving sugar. Continue to stir while bringing everything to a rolling boil and continue boiling for 30 minutes.

To sterilize the jars, fill with boiling water, let stand for 5 minutes and discard the water.

Put the hot preserve into the jars and close immediately.

Spiced pickled rhubarb

Prep and cook time: 45 minutes
Cannot be frozen
Makes: 3 large jars

Ingredients:
500 ml | 2 cups dry white wine
400 g | 1 lb sugar
1 tbsp freshly grated ginger
1 tsp grated lemon peel
1 cinnamon stick
8 whole cloves
1 tsp nutmeg
1 ½ kg | 3 lbs rhubarb

Method:
Slowly bring the wine with 2 cups of water and sugar to a boil stirring occasionally.

Add the ginger, grated lemon peel, cinnamon stick, cloves and nutmeg.

Wash and peel the rhubarb. Chop it into chunks.

Add it to the sugar water and bring the contents to a boil. Remove the rhubarb with a slotted spoon.

Fill the jars with the hot fruit.

Over a moderate heat, continue cooking the sugar water for a further 15-20 minutes until it reaches a syrupy consistency.

Pour the hot syrup over the rhubarb so that it is completely covered. Close the jars securely and let cool.

Vegetable chutney

Prep and cook time: 1 hour
Cannot be frozen
Makes: 2 large pint jars

Ingredients:
8 tomatoes
2 red bell peppers, deseeded
and chopped
2 green bell peppers, deseeded
and chopped
2 apples, peeled, cored and chopped
1 red chilli pepper, deseeded
and cut into strips
3 onions, finely chopped
2 garlic cloves, chopped
1 tsp paprika powder
$\frac{1}{2}$ tsp ground cardamom
80 ml | $\frac{1}{3}$ cup white wine vinegar
60 g | $\frac{1}{4}$ cup sugar
$\frac{1}{4}$ tsp salt

Method:
Briefly blanch the tomatoes. Immerse in cold water.
Remove the skins and seeds, and then chop.

Put the tomatoes, peppers, apples, chilli, onions and garlic
in a large pan.

Add the paprika powder, cardamom, vinegar, sugar and salt
and mix well. Bring all the ingredients to a boil.

Reduce the heat and simmer for approximately 40 minutes,
stirring occasionally.

To sterilize the jars fill with boiling water, let stand for 5 minutes
then discard water. Fill the prepared jars with the chutney.
Close tightly and allow to cool.

index

index.

index.